Editor
Walter Kelly, M.A.

Editorial Project Manager
Ina Massler Levin, M.A.

Editor-in-Chief
Sharon Coan, M.S. Ed.

Cover Artist
Jessica Orlando

Art Coordinator
Denice Adorno

Creative Director
Richard D'Sa

Imaging
Alfred Lau
James Edward Grace
Rosa C. See

Product Manager
Phil Garcia

Publishers
Rachelle Cracchiolo, M.S. Ed.
Mary Dupuy Smith, M.S. Ed.

Narrative Writing

Grades 6–8

Written by

Andrea Trischitta, MA, MAT

Teacher Created Materials, Inc.
6421 Industry Way
Westminster, CA 92683
www.teachercreated.com
ISBN-1-57690-994-8

©2000 Teacher Created Materials, Inc.
Reprinted, 2002
Made in U.S.A.

The classroom teacher may reproduce copies of materials in this book for classroom use only. The reproduction of any part for an entire school or school system is strictly prohibited. No part of this publication may be transmitted, stored, or recorded in any form without written permission from the publisher.

Table of Contents

What Is Narrative Writing?

Narrative writing is best defined as a story. You tell stories every day and may not realize it! How was school today? What did you do in science lab? Did you go somewhere after school? How did your meeting with the coach go? Why didn't you finish your homework? What happened at the dance? All of these questions elicit stories—stories with a beginning, middle, and end.

Narratives are usually told in chronological order; each event is unfolded in exactly the order it happened. What differentiates a good narrative from a not-so-good narrative? The way the story is told. How do you describe your characters? Do you make the setting real? Is the conflict strong? Do you use words and phrases to make your listeners feel they are part of the story? When you write narratives, you must keep the same intensity as when orally sharing a story. When you tell a story, you have the power to change your inflection. You can whisper the secrets, scream at the enemies, change voices for different characters, and emphasize the words that need emphasis. When you tell a story, you can use your arms to imitate verbs like *grab* and *crush* or hold your hands up high in fear or shock and use your facial expressions to mimic the characters' reactions. The main difference between an oral story and a written story is that a written story can last forever. Oral stories may last but are changed over time. When you write, remember that your words exist. Your stories will exist. Write with the intensity that you need to tell a story. Make your narratives come alive and exist because of you!

Narrative writing encourages readers to participate in the story. Strong narratives let the readers feel so involved that they feel for the characters and the conflicts they face. This is called *empathy*. When readers empathize with the characters and the situations they face, the reader will also identify with the characters' thoughts and feelings. Personal narratives (narratives written about your own experiences), nonfiction narratives (stories written about actual events and actual people), and fictional narratives (invented stories) let readers experience things they may never otherwise experience; teach readers about someone, something, or an event in a way that readers understand; and provide escape from the reader's world. All narratives share the same components crucial to intriguing narratives: beginning, middle, climax, and end in proper sequence; believable, non-stereotyped characters; vivid settings; accurate point of view; authentic voice; lively, original descriptions; and a message or theme.

What makes a successful story worth writing and reading? First, an interesting story. Chances are that if it interests you, it will also interest your readers. Second, you, as author, must combine and integrate narrative components, manipulate words and sentences, and engage your reader. You must create the story that must be written. You must create the story that needs to be heard.

How to Use Narrative Writing

❑ Introduce *Narrative Writing* by first defining narrative writing. Students should volunteer examples of books, short stories, television shows, and movies that are examples of narratives.

❑ *Narrative Writing* allows both teacher and student to journey through all elements of narrative writing so that the concepts inherent in narrative writing will be understandable and accessible. Personal narratives, nonfiction narratives, narratives about literature, fairy tale narratives, and the short story will be explored. All sections encompass writing projects that follow the writing process. Publishing and technology ideas are provided.

❑ Begin with the components of narrative writing. Students will manipulate conflict, create realistic characters, practice with sensory imagery and figurative language, brainstorm themes, create settings, write effective dialogue, use strong action verbs, utilize transitional words and phrases, and experiment with point of view. When writing narratives, then, students will have had guided practice on each of the elements, along with a writing journal full of ideas and mini-narratives that can be expanded and shaped to meet specific needs of the various narrative writing topics presented in this book.

❑ Review the Writing Process (pages 7 and 8) and share the analogy of how writing is similar to growing a flower garden. Encourage students to illustrate each stage of the writing process, based on the analogy.

❑ *Narrative Writing* emphasizes the prewriting stage of the writing process. In order to get quality narratives, students need to think, plan, research, and internalize the topic. The more that students brainstorm, free-write, cluster, complete graphic organizers, read quality narratives, and gather information, the stronger their narratives will be.

Brainstorming

Clustering

Free-writing

Using Graphic Organizers

Reading Quality Narratives

4   ©2000 Teacher Created Materials, Inc.

Classroom Atmosphere

Metal scraping against linoleum floor, hiccups at three-second intervals, cars whizzing by open windows, lockers slamming, whispers—distractions! The classroom is hardly an ideal environment for writing. However, if the narrative writing assignment is stimulating, students will write and write and write, regardless of the writing environment. The classroom is where students will be introduced to their narrative writing assignments, but during the course of the school day these narrative ideas will be sifted through the subconscious. Personal connections will be made, and questions will be formulated. Ideas will emerge. The narrative writing topic is so compelling that it brews instinctively. When the student sits to meet the narrative assignment head on, the narrative will practically write itself. A story is born.

The writing classroom must be supportive. Students should be comfortable sharing their thoughts and feelings with others without feeling judged, threatened, or singled out. Teachers should share their thoughts and ideas along with students for each writing assignment. By modeling openness, trust is formed—an invaluable trait in the writing classroom. Students will realize that all opinions are valuable and worth sharing. Be receptive to students who want to alter assignments to fit their needs. *Give* high expectations. *Expect* quality work.

Teachers can help make the classroom conducive to writing. By joining in the writing assignments and sharing the prewriting activities with students, the teacher helps the students understand that writing is indeed a process—a process that creates quality writing worth sharing with others.

Everyone can be a writer. Every teacher of writing can also write. Everyone has a story to tell. The atmosphere of the classroom needs to guarantee that the story is worth telling.

One motto in writing classrooms has always been "Show, don't tell." That is what writing teachers need to do to increase the quality of student writing. By engaging in the narrative writing assignments, teachers practice what they preach. By showing involvement and compassion toward those involved in writing, teachers are proving they are strong advocates for writing.

The Writing Journal

Everyone is unique. We all have our habits and quirks. We all have our own writing preferences. Therefore, do not make a certain *type* of writing journal mandatory; rather, simply make a *writing journal* mandatory. Let students take ownership and express their individuality in writing journals, which will house their brainstorms, lists, ideas, prewriting activities, drafts, and doodles.

Writing is a maze. A beginning eventually leads to the end. The writing journal becomes the place for students to make wrong turns, to write intense beginnings that lead nowhere, to have characters they initially want to do one thing but eventually do another, and to find their way through the maze.

The important concept is that students should have only one journal where all writing goes. Teachers should keep writing portfolios, and students should be given (under teacher protection) their own computer discs to store narratives.

Students often want teachers to read their personal journals. With bulging class sizes, there is never enough time to read and respond to journals or narratives, as well as meet the other demands placed on teachers. Nevertheless, if a student wants his or her teacher to read a journal, this is the highest compliment a teacher can receive, and the journal should be read. Have each student earmark three pages of his or her personal journal for you to read, and then you can respond either in the journal or orally. By achieving the trust of the class and being a part of the writing process, you will find the writing assignments become a pleasure to read.

Your students (except for that handful!) will write from the heart and will tell the story—the story that needs to be shared.

The Writing Portfolio

Each student should have a writing portfolio (manila folders are perfect). Students may like to decorate the front cover, perhaps an "All About Me" collage. The writing portfolio should be kept in the classroom, housing all final copies (including unfinished drafts that didn't have the oomph to reach their end), and be accessible so students may return to even the final narratives and revise.

Because most schools and homes now have word processors, it is easy to print two copies, one for the writing portfolio and one for the refrigerator. Writing portfolios can go home with the student at the end of the year or be passed on to the next writing instructor. Whatever the case may be, urge students to save their work—save, as in *forever*. Over the course of the year, students may return to selections they previously thought weak and revise or gain a new perspective of their "final" drafts and choose to revise.

The Writing Process

Prewriting

In the prewriting stage most of the work is actually done. The first step is thinking: an assignment is given or narrative topics are brainstormed, and before pencil greets paper, ideas, thoughts, words, memories, and stories flow through the mind. Chances are, one idea will escape and end up somewhere near the student's heart—it is this idea that lingers. So, in the lunch line, during passing time, walking home from school . . . this same idea stalks the student; and if the idea isn't unleashed on paper soon, the student may explode.

Before writing, students should make personal connections to the topic. By reflecting on memories and events and recalling them as if they happened yesterday, the students will find that the story awakens. If the topic is nonfiction, students should list what they know and what they don't know. Scavenge for information and find the story's worth. Bring it to life for others. If the narrative is based on literature, students need to put themselves in the story to empathize with the characters and the dilemmas they face.

Ideas for prewriting include brainstorming; free-writing; listing who, what, when, where, why, and how; questioning; creating a "plot jot"; asking and answering questions; listing the parts of your narrative— beginning, middle, climax, and end; identifying conflict, characters, setting, and theme; and establishing point of view. Overwhelming! But remember, the more effort put into prewriting tasks, the easier writing narratives will be.

Compare the prewriting stage to preparing a garden. One cannot throw down seeds or buy established plants and put them in the ground and expect them to look like the picture in gardening catalogues. First, a plan is needed. Type of garden (vegetable, flower, herb, etc.), garden location, quality of soil, germination time, water and sun requirements all affect the quality of the garden. Planning a garden is challenging. If the right plants or locations are not chosen, the plants will not achieve optimum growth. However, planning a garden is fun, and the rewards can be great.

Writing

Flowers and seeds are planted according to the plan. Nature cannot be expected to do the rest. Although the plants may be thriving in their new home, overwatering, lack of fertilizer, or underwatering can affect the plants' health and survival.

This stage parallels the second stage of the writing process, the actual writing of the narrative.

Students brainstorm, jot down ideas, create characters, develop setting and conflict, and establish point of view. Information is gathered and outlined sequentially. Now it's time to write! Write, write, write. Once words flow, write: beginning, middle, and end. There, the narrative is done.

If the characters do not seem to have any direction, the theme is not clear, or the conflict is not strong, then perhaps the narrative needs attention. You need to stop and think. Do you care about your narrative? Does it seem worth writing? If you answer "yes," then you need to take a break and look at the narrative with fresh eyes.

The Writing Process *(cont.)*

Revising

The garden grows, just as the narrative has emerged. Is it over? No. The garden flourishes, but some flowers need to be thinned, and some areas are sparse. Grab the trowel and dig! Rearrange here and there, add fertilizer, check for bugs, dead-head spent flowers, and put mulch down to prevent weeds.

At the revision stage, the job is to add, omit, read, reread, and share with friends, classmates, teacher, and family to elicit comments and suggestions. The more feedback, the better—but remember that it is impossible to make everyone happy. Aunt Tilly may weep after reading the heart-wrenching personal account of seeing the family pet hit by a delivery truck, but friends may ask, "What kind of pet was it? What was its name?" Oh, that's right—Aunt Tilly gave you the lab/shepherd mix for your eighth birthday, and the dog was named "Cupcake" because that was the year cupcakes were chosen over the standard ice-cream cake. Aunt Tilly knew that. Friends and classmates did not. So, take advice, but consider the source.

Editing

Editing is the next stage of the writing process, and it is similar to weeding. The narrative has been revised, and now is the time to proofread the story for errors, weeds, that may weaken it. Misspelled words, sloppy punctuation errors, and overall laziness can make a good story bad. Take pride in the hard work and effort put into the narrative.

As for the garden, it's maintenance time! Weed, water, and fertilize to keep it in top-notch shape. A great deal of time has been invested, and the support of a gardener is needed.

Publishing

Now is when the narrative is shown off! Gloat, smile, and share the narrative that has involved so much energy, patience, and dedication. Narratives can be presented to the class, e-mailed to friends and family, illustrated, word processed, displayed on a bulletin board, or stuck on the refrigerator. Publishing is the stage of the writing process that allows the author to earn the recognition he or she deserves.

As for the garden—congratulations, the "green thumb" statue is on the family bookshelf. Flowers, vegetables, and herbs provide beauty, food, and a haven for butterflies, ladybugs, and bees. Admire the garden that took so much time and planning. Everyone else will, too.

Gardening and writing narratives are similar. Hard work reaps great rewards.

8

©2000 Teacher Created Materials, Inc.

Narrative Writing Thought Questions

Answer the following questions in your journal, and share responses with your classmates.

❑ What types of stories do you like to read, and why? List types of stories and specific titles. Include why the story was good.

❑ What makes a good story? Try to think of three specific reasons.

❑ Have you ever . . .

   • read a story that starts out well, but you soon find yourself bored? Why?

   • been forced to read a story, and finally, toward the end, said, "Now, it's interesting"?

   • read a story that you didn't understand? Why do you think you didn't understand it?

   • listened to a story that was ruined by how it was presented?

   • listened to a story and been completely bored, even though it may have been read well? Why?

   • listened to a story and been totally engrossed in it? Why?

   • read a book and also seen a movie version of that same book? What book? Which was better—the movie or the book? Why?

❑ What is the most difficult aspect of writing for you?

❑ What do you enjoy most about writing?

❑ What types of stories do you like to write? Why?

❑ Why do you think you need to practice writing?

❑ What are some titles of narrative literature?

Standards for Writing
Grades 6–8

Accompanying the major activities of this book will be references to the basic standards and benchmarks for writing that will be met by successful performance of the activities. Each specific standard and benchmark will be referred to by the appropriate letter and number from the following collection. For example, a basic standard and benchmark identified as **1A** would be as follows:

> **Standard 1: Demonstrates competence in the general skills and strategies of the writing process**
> **Benchmark A: Prewriting:** Uses a variety of prewriting strategies (e.g., makes outlines, uses published pieces as writing models, constructs critical standards, brainstorms, builds background knowledge)

A basic standard and benchmark identified as **4B** would be as follows:

> **Standard 4: Gathers and uses information for research purposes**
> **Benchmark B:** Uses the card catalog to locate books for research topics

Clearly, some activities will address more than one standard. Moreover, since there is a rich supply of activities included in this book, some will overlap in the skills they address, and some, of course, will not address every single benchmark within a given standard. Therefore, when you see these standards referenced in the activities, refer to this section for complete descriptions.

Although virtually every state has published its own standards and every subject area maintains its own lists, there is surprising commonality among these various sources. For the purposes of this book, we have elected to use the collection of standards synthesized by John S. Kendall and Robert J. Marzano in their book *Content Knowledge: A Compendium of Standards and Benchmarks for K–12 Education* (Second Edition, 1997) as illustrative of what students at various grade levels should know and be able to do. The book is published jointly by McRel (Mid-continent Regional Educational Laboratory, Inc.) and ASCD (Association for Supervision and Curriculum Development). (Used by permission of McRel.)

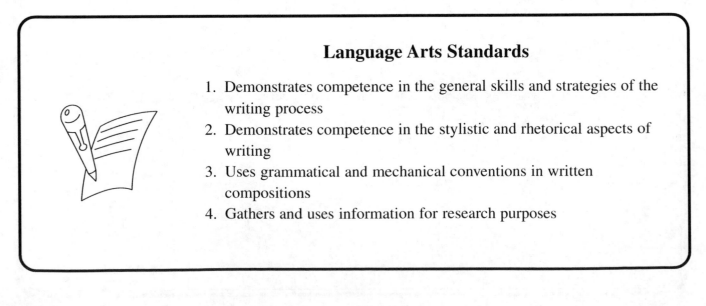

Language Arts Standards

1. Demonstrates competence in the general skills and strategies of the writing process
2. Demonstrates competence in the stylistic and rhetorical aspects of writing
3. Uses grammatical and mechanical conventions in written compositions
4. Gathers and uses information for research purposes

Standards for Writing
Grades 6–8 *(cont.)*

Level III

> **1. Demonstrates competence in the general skills and strategies of the writing process**

    A. Prewriting: Uses a variety of prewriting strategies (e.g., makes outlines, uses published pieces as writing models, constructs critical standards, brainstorms, builds background knowledge)

    B. Drafting and Revising: Uses a variety of strategies to draft and revise written work (e.g., analyzes and clarifies meaning, makes structural and syntactical changes, uses an organizational scheme, uses sensory words and figurative language, rethinks and rewrites for different audiences and purposes, checks for a consistent point of view and for transitions between paragraphs, uses direct feedback to review compositions)

    C. Editing and Publishing: Uses a variety of strategies to edit and publish written work (e.g., eliminates slang; edits for grammar, punctuation, capitalization, and spelling at a developmentally appropriate level; proofreads using reference materials, word processor, and other resources; edits for clarity, word choice, and language usage; uses a word processor to publish written work)

    D. Evaluates own and others' writing (e.g., applies criteria generated by self and others, uses self-assessment to set and achieve goals as a writer, participates in peer response groups)

    E. Uses style and structure appropriate for specific audiences (e.g., public, private) and purposes (e.g., to entertain, to influence, to inform)

    F. Writes expository compositions (e.g., presents information that reflects knowledge about the topic of the report, organizes and presents information in a logical manner)

    G. Writes narrative accounts (e.g., engages the reader by establishing a context and otherwise developing reader interest; establishes a situation, plot, persona, point of view, setting, and conflict; creates an organizational structure that balances and unifies all narrative aspects of the story; uses sensory details and concrete language to develop plot and character; excludes extraneous details and inconsistencies; develops complex characters; uses a range of strategies such as dialogue, tension or suspense, naming, and specific narrative action such as movement, gestures, and expressions)

    H. Writes compositions about autobiographical incidents (e.g., explores the significance and personal importance of the incident, uses details to provide a context for the incident, reveals personal attitude towards the incident, presents details in a logical manner)

    I. Writes biographical sketches (e.g., illustrates the subject's character using narrative and descriptive strategies such as relevant dialogue, specific action, physical description, background description, and comparison or contract to other people; reveals the significance of the subject to the writer; presents details in a logical manner)

    J. Writes persuasive compositions (e.g., engages the reader by establishing a context, creating a persona, and otherwise developing reader interest; develops a controlling idea that conveys a judgment; creates and organizes a structure appropriate to the needs and interests of a specific audience; arranges details, reasons, examples, and/or anecdotes persuasively; excludes information and arguments that are irrelevant; anticipates and addresses reader concerns and counter-arguments; supports arguments with details and evidence, citing sources of appropriate information)

Standards for Writing
Grades 6–8 *(cont.)*

K. Writes compositions that speculate on problems/solutions (e.g., identifies and defines a problem in a way appropriate to the intended audience, describes at least one solution, presents logical and well-supported reasons)

L. Writes in response to literature (e.g., anticipates and answers a reader's questions, responds to significant issues in a log or journal, answers discussion questions, writes a summary of a book, describes an initial impression of a text, connects knowledge from a text with personal knowledge)

M. Writes business letters and letters of request and response (e.g., uses business letter format; states purpose of the letter; relates opinions, problems, requests, or compliments; uses precise vocabulary)

2. Demonstrates competence in the stylistic and rhetorical aspects of writing

A. Uses descriptive language that clarifies and enhances ideas (e.g., establishes tone and mood, uses figurative language)

B. Uses paragraph form in writing (e.g., arranges sentences in sequential order, uses supporting and follow-up sentences)

C. Uses a variety of sentence structures to express expanded ideas

D. Uses some explicit transitional devices

3. Uses grammatical and mechanical conventions in written compositions

A. Uses simple and compound sentences in written compositions

B. Uses pronouns in written compositions (e.g., relative, demonstrate, personal, [i.e., possessive, subject, object])

C. Uses nouns in written compositions (e.g., forms possessive of nouns, forms irregular plural nouns)

D. Uses verbs in written compositions (e.g., uses linking and auxiliary verbs, verb phrases, and correct forms of regular and irregular verbs)

E. Uses adjectives in written compositions (e.g., pronominal, positive, comparative, superlative)

F. Uses adverbs in written compositions (e.g., chooses between forms of adjectives and adverbs)

G. Uses prepositions and coordinating conjunctions in written compositions (e.g., uses prepositional phrases, combines and embeds ideas using conjunctions)

H. Uses interjections in written compositions

I. Uses conventions of spelling in written compositions (e.g., spells high-frequency, commonly misspelled words from appropriate grade-level list; uses a dictionary and other resources to spell words, uses common prefixes and suffixes as aids to spelling; applies rules for irregular structural changes)

J. Uses conventions of capitalization in written compositions (e.g., titles: books, stories, poems, magazines, newspapers, songs, works of art; proper nouns: team names, companies, schools and institutions, departments of government, religions, school subjects; proper adjectives: nationalities, brand names of products)

Standards for Writing
Grades 6–8 *(cont.)*

K. Uses conventions of punctuation in written compositions (e.g., uses exclamation marks after exclamatory sentences and interjections; uses decimal points in decimal, dollars and cents; uses commas with nouns of address and after mild interjections; uses quotation marks with poems, songs, and chapters; uses colons in business letter salutations; uses hyphens to divide words between syllables at the end of a line)

L. Uses standard format in written compositions (e.g., includes footnotes; uses italics for titles of books, magazines, plays, movies)

4. Gathers and uses information for research purposes

A. Gathers data for research topics from interviews (e.g., prepares and asks relevant questions, makes notes of responses, compiles responses)

B. Uses the card catalog to locate books for research topics

C. Uses the *Reader's Guide to Periodical Literature* and other indexes to gather information for research topics

D. Uses a computer catalog to gather information for research topics

E. Uses a variety of sources to gather information for research topics (e.g., magazines, newspapers, dictionaries, schedules, journals, directories, globes, atlases, almanacs)

F. Determines the appropriateness of an information source for a research topic

G. Organizes information and ideas from multiple sources in systematic ways (e.g., time lines, outlines, notes, graphic representations)

H. Writes research papers (e.g., separates information into major components based on a set of criteria, examines critical relationships between and among elements of a research topic, integrates a variety of information into a whole)

Conflict

This section of *Narrative Writing* is composed of 13 separate but interlocking parts: conflict, characterization, setting, verbs, dialogue, theme, transitions, the four W's + H, story structure, plot jots, figurative language, sensory imagery, and tools for writing. Specific examples and lessons are included for each part so that models and practice are available for instruction and review. All 13 components are important to effective narrative writing, none being insignificant. For our purposes, however, it might be said that without conflict there would probably not be any true narrative writing. There could be writing, yes—even excellent writing. But without conflict, that writing might better be classified as descriptive or expository. So we begin our study of narrative writing with conflict.

Conflict is the problem or obstacle the character is trying to overcome. Without conflict, our stories, as well as our lives, would be somewhat boring. Why?

For one thing, what story would be interesting without conflict? When we read, we cheer for the character, hoping he or she will triumph over the various conflicts. Often, there is more than one conflict, which keeps us on the edge of our seats and makes us ask, "and *then* what happened?"

We have all dreamed of having a problem-free life. But what would happen if we never were confronted with a problem? Initially, we would be happy in our Utopian world. In time, however, life would become dull and monotonous. Would we be motivated to achieve higher levels? Probably not. By surviving and overcoming conflicts, we learn to believe in ourselves and to attack future conflicts with confidence.

Think about your favorite books. What were the obstacles or conflicts confronting the main characters? How would the narrative have changed if there were no conflicts?

Take Theodore Taylor's *The Cay,* for example. The conflicts are many: World War II, Phillip's boat being torpedoed, Phillip and Timothy lost at sea, Phillip losing his sight, Phillip and Timothy surviving on an island, Timothy's death, Phillip's survival on the island alone. As you can see, there is more than one conflict in *The Cay*. However, the main conflict of *The Cay* is overcoming prejudice. Timothy is black and Phillip is white. Phillip's blindness finally allows him to see that people are equal, regardless of the color of their skin.

In *The Cay*, the faster one conflict is resolved, the sooner a new conflict raises its head. The series of conflicts makes the pages of the book turn by themselves. Not many of us share the experience of being in a war, being stranded on an island with a stranger who then dies, and being afflicted with no eyesight for over four months. But we do understand prejudice. Theodore Taylor makes Phillip's adventure real, so we not only empathize with his trials but also his realizations and triumphs.

Conflict is needed for good stories, and as seen in the deceptively simple *The Cay*, the conflict is often richer and more complex than we might suspect. In fact, all human behavior in one way or another contains conflict of some type. It is a good writer's job to show us this in his or her narratives.

 **Standards and Benchmarks:** 1A, 1K

Conflict *(cont.)*

Conflict Types

There are many types of conflict, and they might easily arise from simple situations. Examine the following examples.

Person vs. Person

You are at the laundromat and are about to put your clothes into the last dryer available when someone else beats you there. What do you do?

Person vs. Machine

The washing machine has finished its cycles, but the only clothes dryer available is out of order. What do you do?

Person vs. Nature

Since the dryer is out of order, you hang the soaking wet clothes on the clothesline. It starts to rain. Now what?

Person vs. Self

When doing the wash, you carelessly mixed the colored clothes with the whites, and you used hot water. As a result, your family's light clothes are streaked, spotted, and ruined. What next?

Person vs. Society

You decide to protest the town ordinance of allowing only one laundromat. You are met with great opposition, as most residents would like a playground at the site you proposed for the new laundromat.

As you can see, laundry day has presented this character with conflict after conflict. Rarely do stories have just one conflict, just as each new day generally brings us several new conflicts. Sometimes conflicts are resolved quickly; others take days, weeks, even years. Unfortunately, as one conflict ends, another usually takes its place.

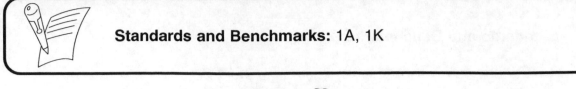

Standards and Benchmarks: 1A, 1K

Conflict *(cont.)*

Conflicts in Various Settings

As a class, generate a list of conflicts from all categories for the following places.

Conflict	Ice-Cream Shop	School Dance
Person vs. Person		
Person vs. Machine		
Person vs. Nature		
Person vs. Self		
Person vs. Society		

Standards and Benchmarks: 1A, 1G

Conflict *(cont.)*

Today's Conflicts

List the conflicts that have arisen today. (The conflicts may or may not be resolved yet. If a conflict has not yet been resolved, predict how it will be.)

Conflict 1: _____

Type of conflict: _____

How the conflict was resolved or prediction of how it will be resolved: _____

_____

Conflict 2: _____

Type of conflict: _____

How the conflict was resolved or prediction of how it will be resolved: _____

_____

Conflict 3: _____

Type of conflict: _____

How the conflict was resolved or prediction of how it will be resolved: _____

_____

Conflict 4: _____

Type of conflict: _____

How the conflict was resolved or prediction of how it will be resolved: _____

_____

Conflict 5: _____

Type of conflict: _____

How the conflict was resolved or prediction of how it will be resolved: _____

_____

Standards and Benchmarks: 1A, 1B, 1C, 1D, 1E, 1G, 1H, 2A, 2B, 2C, 2D, 3A, 3B, 3C, 3D, 3E, 3F, 3G, 3H, 3I, 3J, 3K, 3L

Conflict *(cont.)*

Personal Past Conflicts

Give five examples of conflicts in your past—one from each category—and explain how each was resolved.

Person vs. Person

Conflict: _____

How the conflict was resolved: _____

_____

Person vs. Machine

Conflict: _____

How the conflict was resolved: _____

_____

Person vs. Nature

Conflict: _____

How the conflict was resolved: _____

_____

Person vs. Self

Conflict: _____

How the conflict was resolved: _____

_____

Person vs. Society

Conflict: _____

How the conflict was resolved: _____

_____

Choose one conflict from above and compose a personal narrative paragraph. Include the circumstances and details of the conflict and the steps you took to resolve it.

 **Standards and Benchmarks:** 1A, 1B, 1C, 1D, 1E, 1G, 1I, 2A, 2B, 2C, 2D, 3A, 3B, 3C, 3D, 3E, 3F, 3G, 3H, 3I, 3J, 3K, 3L

Conflict *(cont.)*

Past and Present Conflicts

Conflict is all around us. Conflict happens to everybody, everywhere, in the past, present, and future. In groups, think of news events from the past for the various types of conflicts. Provide explanations of how the conflict was resolved. Next, think of current event conflicts. If the conflict has not yet been resolved, predict the outcome.

Conflict	Past Event	Resolution
Person vs. Person		
Person vs. Machine		
Person vs. Nature		
Person vs. Self		
Person vs. Society		

Conflict	Current Event	Resolution
Person vs. Person		
Person vs. Machine		
Person vs. Nature		
Person vs. Self		
Person vs. Society		

Share your "in the news" conflicts with your class. Choose one from which to write a nonfiction narrative. Include the circumstances leading up to the conflict, and tell how the conflict was resolved or may be resolved.

Standards and Benchmarks: 1A, 1B, 1C, 1D, 1E, 1F, 1G, 1I, 2A, 2B, 2C, 2D, 3A, 3B, 3C, 3D, 3E, 3F, 3G, 3H, 3I, 3J, 3K, 3L, 4A, 4B, 4C, 4D, 4E, 4F, 4G, 4H

Conflict *(cont.)*

Famous People Conflicts

Superstars did not reach their status without stumbling along the way. Discovering their respective conflicts and how they overcame them makes us appreciate their successes all the more. Take Michael Jordan, the basketball great. Did you know he didn't make his high school basketball team at first? Walt Disney, creator of fabulous movies and theme parks, was told that he had no imagination by one of his teachers. Albert Einstein had great difficulty in school but persevered and is today a universally recognized symbol of genius.

Think of five entertainers, athletes, and/or business or historical figures whom you find interesting. Working in groups, research at least one conflict these persons had to overcome prior to achieving fame and at least one conflict these persons had to overcome after achieving fame.

Name of Person and Occupation	Conflict Before Fame	Conflict After Fame
1) _____ source of information: _____		
2) _____ source of information: _____		
3) _____ source of information: _____		
4) _____ source of information: _____		
5) _____ source of information: _____		

As a group, compose a nonfiction narrative paragraph based on one of your celebrities or recognized figures. Write about one past and one present conflict, telling how the first was resolved and how you think the second will or can be resolved.

 **Standards and Benchmarks:** 1A, 1B, 1C, 1D, 1E, 1G, 1H, 2A, 2B, 2C, 2D, 3A, 3B, 3C, 3D, 3E, 3F, 3G, 3H, 3I, 3J, 3K, 3L, 4A, 4G

Conflict *(cont.)*

Relative Conflicts

Remember your relatives! How did conflict shape their lives?

Interview at least two family members. Ask family members to share one conflict they have triumphed over and one conflict which defeated them. Define the type of conflict. Choose one family member to write two narrative paragraphs about. The first paragraph should describe the circumstances which initiated the first conflict and how it was successfully overcome. The second paragraph should retell events leading up to Conflict 2 and how it was resolved, but not in your relative's favor.

❑ **Relative 1:** _____

Conflict 1: _____

Type of conflict: _____

How the conflict was resolved:_____

_____

Conflict 2: _____

Type of conflict: _____

How the conflict was resolved:_____

_____

❑ **Relative 2:** _____

Conflict 1: _____

Type of conflict: _____

How the conflict was resolved:_____

_____

Conflict 2: _____

Type of conflict: _____

How the conflict was resolved:_____

_____

Standards and Benchmarks: 1A, 1B, 1C, 1D, 1E, 1F, 1G, 1H, 1L, 2A, 2B, 2C, 2D, 3A, 3B, 3C, 3D, 3E, 3F, 3G, 3H, 3I, 3J, 3K, 3L

Conflict *(cont.)*

The Hardest Words to Say

In my family, the words "I love you" are never said. It's not that we don't love each other; we just never say it. Kind of like our own version of the kindergarten game "show and tell." Because we do show that we love each other every day. I help my sister learn her numbers, and I collect my baby sister's peas from under her chair. My mom puts oatmeal raisin cookies in my lunch, and my dad takes me to the tractor-pull exhibitions. So, we do love each other.

Then the puppy came. Everyone oohed and ahhed over the puppy, and I've never heard "I love you" so much. I even said it. Plus, I said "I love you" in front of people. "Oh, I love my new puppy, you should just see him!" I'd exclaim. And Shadow would nip my fingers, and I'd scratch between his ears until he got all droopy-eyed and flopped at my feet.

My sister squealed, "I la-la-la-love you, Shadow!" She never said that when we practiced the alphabet two thousand times so that I heard it in my sleep.

"Lovey Dovey Shadow," crooned Mom, "Where's my Lovey Dovey Shadow?" And she practically held his aluminum dog bowl while Shadow slopped food all over the kitchen floor. My mom didn't make Shadow finish every last crumb. She simply said, "Not hungry, my love? Maybe you will finish later."

When my dad came home, he'd shout, "Where's my boy, where's my boy?" Shadow would gallop in and run between his legs a million times.

At night, with Shadow curled into a ball at the foot of my bed, I even whispered, "Good night, Shadow, I love you." It felt wonderful to say those three words. Somehow, I slept better after saying them. It felt wonderful to show and tell love.

Last night, after my mom and dad squished the covers under my neck, and my mom kissed me on the nose, and Dad tousled my hair, I murmured, "I love you."

Their silhouettes froze in the doorway.

I suddenly hoped they hadn't heard me. I could see my heart beating through my covers, and rolled over so my blanket shielded my eyes. Somehow I managed to fall asleep.

22

©2000 Teacher Created Materials, Inc.

Conflict *(cont.)*

The Hardest Words to Say *(cont.)*

The next day was business as usual. Grab the lunch bag, go to school, home, play, eat, homework. Dad came home early, and shouted, "Where's my boy?" I bit the inside of my lip and continued playing "Go Fish" with my sister. Of course, Shadow galloped from his hiding spot and ran in and out of Dad's legs. I couldn't concentrate on the cards in my hand and, for once, did not care that my sister matched cards that didn't match.

Dad sat down on the floor and hugged me. "No, here's my boy." Then he said, "I love you, Jonah. I love you."

My mother sat down with us and sorted the cards, but looked first at me and my sister. "You know I love you both, more than you can ever imagine." Tears trickled down her cheeks.

"Oh, Mommy, you are silly!" my sister giggled.

"Hey," my dad said, "how about you and me pitching some balls at the park?"

"Sure!" I grabbed my baseball glove from the closet and tossed my father the ball. "Where's Shadow's leash? He loves chasing balls."

"No, this is our time, Jonah, you and me." My dad and I walked to the door. Shadow tripped over his tail, he was so excited.

"Ah, Dad, can't we bring Shadow? He loves the park!" I begged. "Just look at him."

"If you want to, Jonah," Dad answered.

I grabbed Shadow's leash, and the three of us headed to the park. After all, how could I go without the one who showed us how to truly express love?

Discussion Questions
- What is the conflict in "The Hardest Words to Say"?
- How is the conflict resolved?
- Identify figurative language in the narrative and discuss how it contributes to the story.

Writing Activities
- Write a personal narrative about love. The conflict should be clear, and the conflict should be resolved.
- Write a dialogue between the mother and/or father and Jonah discussing the phrase "I love you."

 **Standards and Benchmarks:** 1A, 1B, 1C, 1D, 1E, 1F, 1G, 1H, 2A, 2B, 2C, 2D, 3A, 3B, 3C, 3D, 3E, 3F, 3G, 3H, 3I, 3J, 3K, 3L

Conflict *(cont.)*

Writing About Conflict

Following are six activities which are ideal for small-group or large-group interaction. The natural focus is on the conflict situations—situations almost guaranteed to provoke interest, discussions, and sometimes role-playing that lead naturally into writing. The writing and dialogue produced will almost automatically be filled with drama and intensity. Moreover, the attention to the resolution of the conflicts will lead students to generate increased confidence in their own abilities to meet conflict, along with developing and mastering writing skills.

1. Provide students with children's books. Students should identify conflicts in narratives, including the types of conflicts. Let them present the conflicts to the class and describe how each conflict was resolved.

2. Students should brainstorm conflicts they have had with friends. In a narrative paragraph, they each should describe the events leading up to such a conflict and tell how the conflict was resolved.

3. Students should brainstorm conflicts they have had with family members. In a narrative paragraph, they each should describe the events leading up to such a conflict and tell how the conflict was resolved.

4. Students should think of a time when they were confronted with a conflict of any type that was not resolved in a manner they desired. They should write about this conflict and its resolution. They may share within peer groups and ask for advice on what might have been done to reach a favorable outcome. They should then write a second narrative paragraph with a proposed solution and share their narratives with the class.

5. On an index card, students should anonymously write one personal conflict which has not been resolved. Place the index cards on a bulletin board and number them. As a class, first define the types of conflict and then offer suggestions to overcome these conflicts. Students may write their advice in the form of a letter.

6. With a partner, students should write and present a conflict dialogue using one of the following conflict situations:

   • a kid and a security officer over an attempted shoplifting

   • two students over a homework issue

   • a cafeteria worker and a student

   • a kid and parent over a school social event

Remember to describe how the conflict unfolds. Let the conflict reach a climax and, finally, a resolution. Even though these are fictional narratives, they must be realistic.

Characterization

When writing narratives, it is essential to develop your characters, fictional or nonfictional. What you envision in your mind must be conveyed to your readers. Good writers will create actual pictures of the characters so they become "real" to their readers.

In Narratives . . .

In narratives, characters need to be realistic. One way of achieving this is to complete a character sketch for each character. The more you know about your character, the more your readers will appreciate him or her as being authentic. You may not use all the information in your character sketch. The important thing is that you have created a character so realistic that you now have choices about what you need to reveal in your narrative about this person.

In Nonfiction . . .

In nonfiction, completing a character sketch is valuable because you will be learning details about this person you may not previously have known. Now you can share these "new" details with your readers. Moreover, knowing more about nonfiction characters helps the writer better understand events to be described in his or her narrative. The character sketch can also be used as an aid for taking notes about a person or as a guide for formulating interview questions.

In Literature . . .

In literature, character sketches are important because you can analyze how or why the character was motivated to act the way he or she did. You can also compare and contrast these traits with other characters or show the relationships between characters. Go into as much detail as possible when completing your character sketch. For example, you may wish to use a revealing nickname; for an overweight character, you may note that the person could use an aerobics class; after listing a favorite book, you may observe that the book was read over a three-month period. The more detailed your comments, the better your characters!

Standards and Benchmarks: 1A

Characterization *(cont.)*
Character Sketch Template

Name _____

Date of Birth _____   **Age** _____   **Male/Female** _____

Address _____

Occupation _____

Physical Description

Eyes _____   Height_____   Weight _____

Complexion _____   Hair_____   Clothing _____

Unique Features _____

Personality _____

Speech_____

Behavior _____

Emotional State _____

Motivation _____

Talents _____

Hobbies _____

	Favorite	**Least Favorite**
Food		
Place		
Book		
Pastime		
Television Show		
Sport		

Family Description
  Name(s) _____
  Age(s) _____
  Relationship(s) to Character _____
  Occupation(s) _____
Home Description _____
Best Friends
  Names_____
  Ages _____
  Traits That Make This Person a Friend _____

Standards and Benchmarks: 1A, 1B, 1C, 1D, 1E, 1F, 1G, 1H, 2A, 2B, 2C, 2D, 3A, 3B, 3C, 3D, 3E, 3F, 3G, 3H, 3I, 3J, 3K, 3L

Characterization *(cont.)*

Personal Character Sketch

1. Complete a character sketch of yourself. Be truthful! Think of one physical attribute you would like to change if you could. Cluster that word in your journal. Write a narrative paragraph about what you would like to see altered, and why. Next, imagine that the physical attribute has been magically changed. How has this change affected your life?

2. As a class, brainstorm a list of adjectives used to describe people. Write these on the board and copy them in a notebook (e.g., *silly, handsome, beautiful, homely, obese, shallow, well-dressed, neat, tiresome, overbearing, rude, smart,* etc.). From this list, you should choose four qualities you possess. Next, you should separately cluster these four qualities. Then compose four narrative paragraphs showing these qualities through actions. The specific adjective itself *must not appear* in the paragraph!

3. Introduce yourself in one paragraph, choosing at least five pieces of information from your personal character sketch. You may not say, "My name is _____. I am _____ years old. My favorite food is _____," etc. The information must be revealed in an intriguing way.

Sample Paragraph

> When I hear the announcer call, "Number 14, Tim Roberts!" I bolt to my position on the field. Those chocolate cupcakes I always eat before a game flip-flop in my stomach, but soon enough, when I hear the whistle, I call the play: "33-24-Hut!" And I forget about everything else but the game.

Based on the above example, what is revealed about the person?

4. Exchange personal character sketches with a peer. Complete the same assignment above. Choose five pieces of information you find intriguing about your classmate and write a narrative paragraph revealing these details (except for the name, of course) without stating them obviously. Read your paragraphs to the class. Can they correctly identify the classmate you are describing?

Standards and Benchmarks: 1A, 1B, 1C, 1D, 1E, 1F, 1G, 1H, 2A, 2B, 2C, 2D, 3A, 3B, 3C, 3D, 3E, 3F, 3G, 3H, 3I, 3J, 3K

Setting

The *setting* is the environment in which the story takes place. It is important to include descriptions of the setting in narratives so the readers can see where the action takes place.

My Favorite Room

Draw or sketch a floor plan of your house. Write a narrative paragraph describing your favorite room in detail. Next, describe your least favorite room.

The Perfect Vacation

Describe your ideal vacation spot. First, brainstorm what makes a great vacation. Draw your vacation spot. In one narrative paragraph, tell why this place is the ideal vacation destination. Create a collage of your vacation spot and present it to the class.

I Have to Go Where?

Make a list of all the places you don't like to go, with reasons why. Choose one of these awful places and compose a narrative paragraph revealing why this place is not high on your "fun-places-to-visit" list. Read the narrative to the class.

Out of This World

Create a new planet in our galaxy. Draw the planet's shape, size, and color, and hang it from the ceiling with string to create a far-out classroom! Then describe this new planet. Read the description to the class.

Games People Play

Describe a sports setting: stadium, diamond, rink, arena, garden, auditorium, etc. Explain not only what it looks like, but also what type of sport is played there. This description and explanation should be addressed to someone who has just arrived on Earth.

 **Standards and Benchmarks:** 1A, 1B, 1C, 2A, 2B, 2C, 2D, 3A, 3B, 3C, 3D, 3E, 3F, 3G, 3H, 3I, 3J, 3K

Setting *(cont.)*

Adding Description

For each of the following sentences, add three more sentences to enhance the setting. Then write one descriptive paragraph for each setting. Each paragraph should have a strong topic sentence, at least three supporting sentences to strengthen and prove the topic sentence, and a concluding sentence.

Each setting should be accompanied by an illustration.

❑ **The house was old.**

Example: Chipped yellow windows seemed to hold up the dilapidated roof all on their own.

_____

_____

_____

_____

❑ **At dusk, the city came alive.**

_____

_____

_____

_____

❑ **The fairgrounds were ready to open.**

_____

_____

_____

_____

❑ **School was chaos.**

_____

_____

_____

_____

 **Standards and Benchmarks:** 1A, 1B, 1C, 1G, 2A, 2B, 2C, 2D, 3A, 3B, 3C, 3D, 3E, 3F, 3G, 3H, 3I, 3J, 3K

Verbs

Verbs are vital to your sentences and narratives. Without verbs, there would be no action, no feeling, no expressing. Without verbs, your stories would not be alive. It is important to choose vivid, strong verbs to create images in your readers' minds.

Connecting Verbs

Picture a busy day in the center of a major city with many different people crossing the street. As an experienced people-watcher, do you find that everyone just "walks" across a street? Absolutely not! Match an appropriate verb below with its owner. A single verb may be used more than once.

1. Elderly man	_____	skipped
2. Baby	_____	boogied
3. Boy	_____	shuffled
4. Girl	_____	scurried
5. Mother	_____	ran
6. Businessman	_____	strutted
7. Athlete	_____	crawled
8. Model	_____	marched
9. Student with boom box	_____	strolled
10. Ballerina	_____	sauntered
11. Squirrel	_____	sprinted

For each "match" below, create a descriptive sentence showing why he or she is crossing the street. Number one has been done for you as an example.

1. The elderly man *shuffled across the street with one red rose he was bringing to his wife for their anniversary.*

2. The baby _____

3. The boy _____

4. The girl _____

5. The mother _____

6. The businessman _____

7. The athlete _____

8. The model _____

9. The student with the boom box _____

10. The ballerina _____

11. The squirrel _____

Select your best sentence and turn it into a one-paragraph narrative. Read the narrative to the class.

Standards and Benchmarks: 1A, 1B, 1C, 1D, 1E, 1G, 2A, 2B, 2C, 2D, 3A, 3B, 3C, 3D, 3E, 3F, 3G, 3H, 3I, 3J, 3K

Verbs *(cont.)*

"Said," Again?

One of the most overused verbs is "said." As a class, brainstorm a list of words to replace "said." Think of how people express themselves. You may find that rarely anything is simply "said." Rather, words, sentences, and thoughts are *breathed, muttered, shouted, revealed, cried, whispered, growled, added,* etc. Students should copy the brainstormed list in their notebooks for reference.

In the following dialogue, change all the "saids." You must not repeat the same word twice.

> "Get back here!" said my mother.
> "No," I said. "All the kids are going to the dance."
> "When your homework is finished," my mother said.
> "It is," I said. "Look on the kitchen table."
> "I don't see anything," my mother said.
> "In my notebook," I said. "Goodbye!"
> "Okay," my mom said, "You be home by nine o'clock, sharp!"
> "Ma, the dance is from eight to ten!" I said.
> "Nine o'clock!" my mom said.

Write variations of verbs on the chalkboard. Remember that there are no single "correct" answers, but the choice of the verb can change the tone of the dialogue. Discuss how different verbs change the meaning of a particular sentence.

For example, in the first line above, the mother could *scream,* "Get back here!" But if the mother *wept,* "Get back here!" the tone changes.

Now, rewrite the dialogue with strong verbs. Also, complete a character sketch on both the mother and her teenager so that in your revisions you reveal details. Continue the dialogue, again not using the word *said.* Share your revisions with the class.

Rewritten Dialogue

_____

_____

_____

_____

_____

_____

Standards and Benchmarks: 1A, 1B, 1C, 1D, 1E, 1G, 2A, 2B, 2C, 2D, 3A, 3B, 3C, 3D, 3E, 3F, 3G, 3H, 3I, 3J, 3K

Verbs *(cont.)*

Verbs in Various Settings

For the following list of places, think of five action verbs you may use in that setting. Next to each verb, develop the action verb in a few (two or three) sentences.

For example: **Garden**

Action Verb—*weed:* I hate weeding my mom's vegetable garden, but if I don't "participate," as she says, then I won't get to eat any tomatoes or corn when they're ready. It seems like I could weed forever and never be done.

❑ **Barnyard**

    Action Verb 1— _____ _____
_____

    Action Verb 2— _____ _____
_____

    Action Verb 3— _____ _____
_____

    Action Verb 4— _____ _____
_____

    Action Verb 5— _____ _____
_____

❑ **Airport**

    Action Verb 1— _____ _____
_____

    Action Verb 2— _____ _____
_____

    Action Verb 3— _____ _____
_____

    Action Verb 4— _____ _____
_____

    Action Verb 5— _____ _____
_____

Verbs *(cont.)*

Verbs in Various Settings *(cont.)*

❏ **School Cafeteria**

Action Verb 1— _____ _____

_____

Action Verb 2— _____ _____

_____

Action Verb 3— _____ _____

_____

Action Verb 4— _____ _____

_____

Action Verb 5— _____ _____

_____

❏ **Beach**

Action Verb 1— _____ _____

_____

Action Verb 2— _____ _____

_____

Action Verb 3— _____ _____

_____

Action Verb 4— _____ _____

_____

Action Verb 5— _____ _____

_____

Choose one setting from above and develop it into a narrative paragraph, using the action verbs. Not only should strong action verbs be used, but also the setting should create a picture in the readers' minds.

_____

_____

_____

_____

_____

Dialogue

Dialogue in your narratives should sound like real people talking. The words you choose for your characters must have a reason for being in the narrative. The more dialogue you use, the faster paced and more dramatic your story will be. Besides revealing how a character actually talks, dialogue can reveal the following:

❑ **Character**

"I want cookie. Puleez, puleez, Momma! I berry hungy!"
What is revealed about this character? _____

_____

"Don't push, Nadine! He can't swim!"
Information about two characters is revealed here. What? _____

_____

"Look at you—knees all dirty and scraped, hair shading your eyes. Well, when was the last time you actually took a bath?"
What is revealed about the characters?_____

_____

"I don't believe you."
What is this character revealing? _____

_____

"I can't sing well enough to try out for the play."
What conflict is revealed? _____

_____

❑ **Mood**

"My day? Well, Grandpa smoked a pack of cigars right on the pull-out sofa, the air-conditioner broke, and when I tried sleeping on the porch, that hole in the screen must have let in every mosquito in Minneapolis."
What is the mood of this character? _____

_____

❑ **Plot**

"This was like first grade, remember? You and me, singing our hearts out, 'Tomorrow, tomorrow, I'll love ya, tomorrow!' I wonder if you or I will get the lead? Then only one of us will be singing, huh?"
What is the plot of this story?_____

_____

"At night the roller coasters go faster, I bet. See how fast those lights swish—see, swish! Wow. Now that's fast. In the daytime, you don't see that swish, no, you don't. I like riding at night. They make everything faster."
What is revealed about the character as well as the setting? _____

_____

_____

34   *©2000 Teacher Created Materials, Inc.*

Standards and Benchmarks: 1A, 1B, 1C, 1D, 1E, 1G, 2A, 2B, 2C, 2D, 3A, 3B, 3C, 3D, 3E, 3F, 3G, 3H, 3I, 3J, 3K, 3L

Dialogue *(cont.)*

Writing Dialogue

Using the steps below, write a two-person dialogue of no more than one page, using two of the following characters:

- ❑ an elderly person with a hearing aid
- ❑ a clown who is out of work
- ❑ a teenager who has a "straight A" report card
- ❑ a dentist who loves cavities
- ❑ eight-year-old twins who found (and ate) a bag of lollipops
- ❑ a car salesman who lies
- ❑ a parent who works nights
- ❑ a tennis instructor who has a sunburn

1. Choose two characters and complete character sketches for each character. Make the characters real! Give them life!

2. Brainstorm a list of conflicts from each category and choose one conflict for each character. Remember to weave that conflict into the dialogue for that particular character.

3. Create a setting that would realistically place these two individuals in the same place at the same time. Brainstorm a list of possible settings. Choose one setting and write a one-paragraph description.

4. Create a dialogue (no narration allowed!) to tell the story. The conflict must be presented, the setting revealed, and the conflict resolved.

5. Obtain props reflective of the above characters and "perform" dialogues with partners.

Standards and Benchmarks: 1A

Theme

In narratives, both personal and nonfiction, a message or theme is conveyed through the plot. *Plot* is the sequence of events in the narrative. Plot is the story which evolves. *Theme* is what the reader learns from the plot—the characters and how they confront the conflicts presented to them. Themes are rarely stated directly. Usually themes are revealed through careful reading and thought.

In *The Wizard of Oz*, the characters learn things about themselves when the Wizard finally awards them with their "prizes." A new brain (to replace the straw brain) is given to the Scarecrow, a mixture of bran (for "brand" new) and pins and needles (for sharpness). A silk heart is put in the Tin Woodsman's chest, and a green "courage" potion suddenly makes the Cowardly Lion brave. But Dorothy reminds them that even without these tangible awards, they were always intelligent, loving, and courageous. Dorothy realizes that she, too, had the power all along to return to Kansas and did not need the assistance of others. She only had to believe in herself.

The following are themes suitable for *The Wizard of Oz*. Under each theme, think of two examples from the story to support the theme. Also, brainstorm other narratives you may have read that have similar themes.

1. Dreams can reveal truths. _____
   _____

2. Know your leader before you elect that person to office. _____
   _____

3. Listen to weather forecasts. _____
   _____

4. You can achieve anything if you put your mind to it. _____
   _____

5. In order to solve a problem, you must face it directly. _____
   _____

As a class, generate at least two more original themes. Ask yourself, "What did I learn from *The Wizard of Oz?*"

Theme 1:_____
Evidence from story: _____
_____

Theme 2:_____
Evidence from story: _____
_____

Standards and Benchmarks: 1A, 1B, 1C, 1D, 1E, 1G, 1H, 2A, 2B, 2C, 2D, 3A, 3B, 3C, 3D, 3E, 3F, 3G, 3H, 3I, 3J, 3K, 3L

Theme *(cont.)*

The Underground World

When they entered the subway station, they entered a whole different world. Initially, it was the odor that caused the two small boys to crinkle their noses. It was a combination of sweat, garbage, and old medicine. Both boys placed their hands on the concrete pole that held up the underground, and the mother reprimanded through clenched teeth, "Dirty! Don't touch anything!" She reached into her pocket, grabbed a tissue that she used on both boys' fingers, and then stuffed it in her pocket.

The screeching of wheels and the thundering, crashing sound that came from the dark tunnel dragged the boys precariously close to the edge of the platform, scarred with chewing gum patties, dirt, and stains from things no one cared to imagine. The mother held the boys' wrists so firmly that their fingers turned a delicious plum color, but neither dared resist, so deafening yet thrilling the sound.

A beam of light glowed from the tunnel, and everyone on the platform changed positions, as if they could guess where the subway car would stop and where the doors would open. Everyone was wrong. Even the mother. At first glance, there didn't seem to be many waiting for the subway, but when the doors opened, the stampede began. Polite shoving and turn-taking, in and out, rushing to beat the slamming of the doors, wondering if everyone who wanted to get off could, and those who wanted to get on, would! The mother hoisted a lad on each hip, and she pushed through the doors without a moment to spare.

No one wanted to sit next to anyone on the subway. It was one of those rules that was understood. But with every other seat taken, the mother had no choice (as separation was not an option) but to grip a metal pole and let the older boy slide down like a fireman, holding onto the pole with one hand and mother's leg with the other. The younger son nestled like a koala bear, staring at the various people near him. The jolting movements of the swaying subway and the lurching determination—or possibly fear in the mother's eyes—caused one subway rider to command, "Sit."

The gentleman slid next to a toothless woman, who edged toward two businesswomen clinging to their briefcases, void of expression. The mother sat, holding the younger boy on her lap, and the other as close to her as possible.

"Hey, Mommy, look!" the blonde-haired boy shouted over the rumbling.

Since no one ever spoke on the subway, they all just turned their eyes (yet kept their heads still—quite miraculous, actually) in the direction of the innocent pointed finger.

"Yes, honey, shhhh." The mother was the only one who fixated on a billboard directly across from her.

"Mommy, over there!" The boy, without realizing it, had placed one hand on the leg of a burly man with tattoos of snakes and pirate ships painted on his forearm and shoulder. The decorated man did not even flinch and kept his eyes vacant.

Theme *(cont.)*

The Underground World *(cont.)*

"Mommy, look! Children! Just my size!" The boy's elation surpassed the clanking and crashing of the subway car. "They can be my friends! Let's have them come over to play. Please, Mommy. Won't it be fun?"

"Perhaps another day," said the mother, who nonchalantly took his waving arm and held it in her own.

"But they look nice, Mommy. I see it in their eyes!" the boy continued.

The subway careened to a halt. The mother repositioned the youngest in his koala hold, and grabbed her other belonging—her eldest son. She barreled through the stampede, never once looking behind.

The blonde-haired boy waved goodbye to the subway and see-you-soon to his friends. He couldn't wait for them to come over and play.

Discussion Questions

- What is the theme or themes of "The Underground World"?
- How does figurative language contribute to the narrative?

Universal Themes

- Good always triumphs over evil.
- You can achieve anything if you put your mind to it.
- Don't judge a book by its cover.
- The grass is always greener on the other side.

As a class, brainstorm other universal themes and write them on the chalkboard.

Choose three themes from above or from the class list and think of a personal incident which reflects each of these three themes. Now, choose one incident about which to write a narrative. After drafting your narrative, read it to the class. Ask students to share what they learned from your essay.

Proverbs

Proverbs often act as themes. For the following proverbs, write what the proverb really means, and not simply the literal meaning.

- People who live in glass houses shouldn't throw stones.
- Birds of a feather flock together.
- Don't put all your eggs in one basket.
- Too many cooks spoil the broth.
- The early bird catches the worm.
- What goes around comes around.

Choose one proverb and think of one personal event and one current event for which that proverb can serve as the theme. Compose one narrative paragraph for each event. Share with the class.

Transitions

In narratives, events are told as they happened. Key words, called *transitions*, are signals to show the order of how things happened. Transitional words help the reader move from idea to idea by stating or implying the connection between ideas. Transitions keep the pace of the story and keep the reader focused on the order of events.

Transitional Words That Link Thoughts

again	so	furthermore	likewise
also	besides	in addition	moreover
and	further	last	next

Transitional Words That Compare Like Ideas

also	in the same way	similarly
as well as	likewise	resembling

Transitional Words That Contrast Like Ideas

after all	however	on the other hand
although	nevertheless	yet
even though	on the contrary	

Transitional Words That Show Sequence and Time

after	earlier	last
next	later	first, second, third, etc.
before	at the same time	meanwhile
during	while	simultaneously

Transitional Words That Show Cause and Effect

accordingly	consequently	since
due to	then	thus
therefore	as a result	because

Transitional Words That Emphasize

edcertainly	surely	undoubtedly
indeed	to be sure	without a doubt
in fact	truly	

Transitional Words That Summarize

consequently	in conclusion	finally
to sum up	in closing	ultimately

 **Standards and Benchmarks:** 1A, 1B, 1C, 1D, 1E, 1G, 1I, 1L, 2A, 2B, 2C, 2D, 3A, 3B, 3C, 3D, 3E, 3F, 3G, 3H, 3I, 3J, 3K, 3L, 4A, 4B, 4C, 4D, 4E, 4F, 4G, 4H

Transitions *(cont.)*

Touchdown!

In my first baby picture, the football is bigger than me and better looking. Honest! So, ever since I was a baby, I've been raised by three parents—Mom, Dad, and a football. When I teethed, I chewed on a plastic football. My crib comforter was as green as Astroturf, and instead of a blanket, I had a furry brown football. I was like Pavlov's dog because whenever I heard the word "Touchdown!" I would hold my two arms straight up in the air.

So, it surprised no one when at age four I could name the offensive line of the Giants and every quarterback in the NFL.

I loved the Pop Warner football games I played as a kid. And the high school football players became my idols. I had their autographs proudly displayed on my bedroom walls. Those early years were great—everyone played, and everyone was more or less the same size.

After that . . . Welcome to high school! Nature was unkind. I was a shrimp. And I prayed I would grow. I prayed I would grow to be the best and biggest quarterback in football history. Finally, in my junior year, I grew six inches. At last, as a senior I made it to the varsity team. I never was a quarterback, but by now I understood that being a part of the team was good enough, whatever the position. I played my best and was voted MVP. To me, it was my Heisman Trophy.

As a final piece of good luck, I was scouted by a local college to play football. Of course, I accepted. And the first thing I'll pack? Well, my furry brown football that I've had ever since I can remember.

I still love football, and sometimes I love watching a game more than I like playing it. Being with my family on Sunday afternoons, cheering and hollering, is just as exciting as holding the football and running, running, running through the defensive line or catching the ball.

Discussion Questions
- What is the theme of "Touchdown!"?
- Identify some of the transitions in this narrative.
- How do transitions help the flow of the narrative?

Writing Activity
In groups, research an athlete. As a group, find at least one conflict that the athlete had to overcome. Write a brief biographical narrative on this athlete, stating his or her conflict, and how it was resolved. Use transitions to make the story coherent and smoothly flowing.

Athlete: _____

Sport: _____

Known for: _____

Conflict:_____

How conflict was overcome: _____

Standards and Benchmarks: 1A, 1B, 1C, 1D, 1E, 1G, 1H, 2A, 2B, 2C, 2D, 3A, 3B, 3C, 3D, 3E, 3F, 3G, 3H, 3I, 3J, 3K, 3L

Transitions *(cont.)*

A Lifetime of Memories

Reflect upon your life thus far. What memories stand out most? Painful remembrances? Funny times? Embarrassing moments? Angry times? Create a time log and choose one memory from each year of your life. Write the emotion, and describe the event. You will need assistance from parents or relatives for your early years. Ask them to share one particular memory from birth to age three or four—depending upon your memory!

❑ **Birth to Age 1:** _____

_____

❑ **Age 2:** _____

_____

❑ **Age 3:** _____

_____

❑ **Age 4:** _____

_____

❑ **Age 5:** _____

_____

❑ **Age 6:** _____

_____

❑ **Age 7:** _____

_____

❑ **Age 8:** _____

_____

Standards and Benchmarks: 1A, 1B, 1C, 1D, 1E, 1G, 1H, 2A, 2B, 2C, 2D, 3A, 3B, 3C, 3D, 3E, 3F, 3G, 3H, 3I, 3J, 3K, 3L

Transitions *(cont.)*

A Lifetime of Memories *(cont.)*

❑ **Age 9:** _____

_____

❑ **Age 10:** _____

_____

❑ **Age 11:** _____

_____

❑ **Age 12:** _____

_____

❑ **Age 13:** _____

_____

Now that you have completed the time log, piece all the events together, using transitions to move from one emotion to the next, as well as year to year. Word-process your narratives, and boldface or highlight in a different color all transitional words.

A Year in the Life of . . .

Next, choose one year of your life from the list above. Write a well-developed paragraph about the memory from that particular year. For the second paragraph, you will use transitional words to write about another memory that is the opposite emotion. For example, if at age four you have a painful memory of falling off a bike and knocking your front teeth out, you may also have a happy memory of going to a museum with your dad. Your second paragraph should contain sentences using contrasting transitional words.

Transition Identification

Read the following example and circle all transitional words.

When I was four, I hated preschool. Even though I couldn't tell time, I quickly learned that when the big hand was at the 6 and the little hand was at the 11, it was time for me to go home. As a result, when I graduated to kindergarten, I thought I would hate it as well. Because my preschool class had this one kid who constantly picked on me, I imagined this same child would be in kindergarten. Therefore, I cried through the whole bus ride to school. I couldn't believe my mom made me get on that bus. I was shocked, to be sure, when I arrived in my new classroom, to see only a few familiar faces, and no bully! I even asked my new teacher where the others were, and she replied, "Oh, they moved over the summer!" Consequently, kindergarten gave me a whole new perspective about school.

 **Standards and Benchmarks:** 1A, 1B, 1C, 1D, 1E, 1H, 2A, 2B, 2C, 2D, 3A, 3B, 3C, 3D, 3E, 3F, 3G, 3H, 3I, 3J, 3K, 3L

Who, What, Where, When, Why, and How

Using the questions *who, what, where, when, why,* and *how* will provide the basics, or foundation, needed to begin a story. By answering these questions, you can determine whether you have enough ideas to sustain a strong narrative.

Narratives can also be summarized by using the same technique. After reading a narrative, answer the questions: Who was in the narrative? What was the narrative about? Where did the narrative take place? When did the events happen? Why did the characters do what they did? How was the conflict resolved?

Remembering the Past

Think of an event from the past that has affected your life today. Use the 5W + H technique to remember the experience.

- Who _____

  _____

- What _____

  _____

- Where _____

  _____

- When _____

  _____

- Why _____

  _____

- How _____

  _____

Next, summarize the event, using the thoughts and details from the 5W + H list, in one strong paragraph.

Now, consider how that event has shaped who you are today.

Because this happened, I am _____

Proceed with details to show just how that one event has affected you. (You will need to use the back of this page.)

Good Story Structure

A good story has all necessary elements, usually in chronological order and in vivid detail. The essential parts of a story should be included in the order they occurred; otherwise, the structure is changed. Think of a good story as a house.

❑ **Foundation:** A good foundation—setting, characters, and conflict—intrigues the reader and encourages the story to grow. With a solid foundation, the story often evolves magically as the characters take control.

❑ **Walls:** Walls are the action of the story, the introduction of secondary characters, and the intensification of conflict.

❑ **Roof:** The peak of the roof is the climax. In narratives, the climax is the turning point of action, the moment when interest and intensity reach their peak. In *The Wizard of Oz*, the climax is when Dorothy and the Wizard prepare to leave for Kansas and fail.

❑ **Doors and Windows:** These are the resolution. The end of a story sums up how the characters will move forward or adjust to their lives now that the conflict is resolved. The ending provides the "finishing touches" to let the reader know that the characters will survive and move on.

❑ **Additional Features:** Of course, every good house needs some landscaping, plumbing, and electricity. Consider these to be the devices authors use to make the story come alive. Figurative language, sensory imagery, and dialogue all aid in the success of the house, or the narrative.

Standards and Benchmarks: 1A, 1B, 1C, 1D, 1G, 2A, 2B, 2C, 2D, 3A, 3B, 3C, 3D, 3E, 3F, 3G, 3H, 3I, 3J, 3K, 3L

Plot Jot

When you begin narratives and you get that spark in your pencil or mind—wherever those creative thoughts originate—you jot down the plot in your notebook. This spontaneous story idea is a *plot jot*.

When you look at the plot jot again, you realize that it needs detail to become a true narrative that others will want to read. The second step of the plot jot is to question the story. Think of at least 10 questions about your plot jot, and then answer them. The revision process will make a narrative out of the plot jot, and create a story that will interest readers.

Consider this plot jot:

- Sam had a nightmare.
- He woke up worried.
- He could hardly eat breakfast.
- He got dressed, walked to school, and did not accept a ride from Julie.
- When he saw the playground, he hid behind a fence.
- The bell rang, and Sam ran into school.
- Finally, he was safe.

Okay, we now have the "architectural design" of the house. Now we need a foundation to see if the house can be built.

Answer the following questions based on the plot jot, and create a story.

Remember, there are no "right" answers. After the narratives are written, discuss the variations of the same plot jot. Discuss how answers change the narrative.

- What was Sam's nightmare about? _____
  _____

- Why did his nightmare worry him? _____
  _____

- Does Sam often have nightmares? _____
  _____

- Is what he ate for breakfast important? _____
  _____

- What did Sam wear to school? _____
  _____

- Is what he wore important to the story? _____
  _____

 **Standards and Benchmarks:** 1A, 1B, 1C, 1D, 1E, 1G, 2A, 2B, 2C, 2D, 3A, 3B, 3C, 3D, 3E, 3F, 3G, 3H, 3I, 3J, 3K, 3L

Plot Jot *(cont.)*

- Does Sam usually walk to school? _____

_____

- Who is Julie? _____

_____

- Does she usually give Sam rides? _____

_____

- Why doesn't Sam accept a ride from her today? _____

_____

- Why doesn't Sam go on the playground? _____

_____

- Why does he hide? _____

_____

- When the bell rings, why does Sam run into school? _____

_____

- Does Sam like school? _____

_____

- Why does he finally feel safe? _____

_____

- Does Sam usually feel this way, or did his nightmare affect his behavior? _____

_____

- How does Sam manage throughout the day? _____

_____

- Will the nightmare reoccur? _____

_____

Questioning the Plot Jot

What follows is another plot jot. In groups, think of eight to ten questions based on the plot jot. Share your questions with the class. Write all questions on the chalkboard. Individually, answer at least 10 questions of your choosing. Write a one-page narrative. Share your narratives with the class.

Initiate a class discussion on the variations and differences in final narratives based upon the same plot jot. This should be a great example of how writing allows us to be ourselves!

- Molly said she'd be there at eight.
- It was 10:15.
- Notes and books were scattered on the table.
- Lucky slammed his notebook closed.
- "It isn't fair," Lucky muttered.
- He saw an envelope in a book he hadn't opened yet. Although it was sealed, Lucky read the letter.
- "No wonder," he sighed.

 **Standards and Benchmarks:** 1A, 1B, 1C, 1D, 1E, 1G, 2A, 2B, 2C, 2D, 3A, 3B, 3C, 3D, 3E, 3F, 3G, 3H, 3I, 3J, 3K, 3L

Plot Jot *(cont.)*

Create Your Own Plot Jot

Get that creative spark and write six to eight sentences showing the basic plot. In groups, have group members read your plot jot and think of 10 questions (minimum) based on your plot jot. Think of questions for each group member's plot jot. Now, take the questions pertaining to your plot jot and answer them thoughtfully and thoroughly. Write a narrative based on this preparation.

Plot Jot

1. _____
2. _____
3. _____
4. _____
5. _____
6. _____
7. _____
8. _____

Questions Based on Plot Jot

1. _____
2. _____
3. _____
4. _____
5. _____
6. _____
7. _____
8. _____
9. _____
10. _____

Answers

1. _____
2. _____
3. _____
4. _____
5. _____
6. _____
7. _____
8. _____
9. _____
10. _____

Revisions

Return to your groups and share the narratives.

Figurative Language

Figurative language enhances description in narrative writing. Figurative language allows readers to enter the story because you are *showing* them instead of telling them. The most common figures of speech include *simile, metaphor, personification, hyperbole, alliteration*, and *onomatopoeia*.

Simile

A *simile* is a comparison between two unlike things using "like" or "as".
- The spider hung from its web.
- *The spider was suspended from its thread like an acrobat on a tightrope.*

Metaphor

A *metaphor* compares two unlike things without using "like" or "as".
- The toothpicks were next to the appetizers.
- *The toothpicks were toy soldiers, ready to spear the appetizers.*

Personification

Personification gives human characteristics and traits to inanimate objects.
- The wind was loud.
- *The wind whispered through my window, revealing night's secrets.*

Hyperbole

Hyperbole is a gross exaggeration, something that could never happen.
- If she lied to him one more time, he would be furious.
- *If she lied to him one more time, he knew his head would explode.*

Alliteration

Alliteration is the repetition of two or more consonant sounds.
- He said he loved her.
- *Silently sighing, he strongly swept her off her feet.*

Onomatopoeia

Onomatopoeia is a word that imitates sounds.
- The soda can opened.
- *The soda can cracked open with a refreshing fizz.*

---

48   ©*2000 Teacher Created Materials, Inc.*

Standards and Benchmarks: 1A, 1B

Figurative Language *(cont.)*

Clichés

Clichés are phrases that are overused and unoriginal. When writing sentences containing figurative language, try to create new ways of comparing and describing things instead of using clichés.

For the following clichés, create original descriptions using figurative language. First, identify the correct figure of speech. Then, put your new phrase in a complete sentence.

Cliché	Figure of Speech	Original Sentence
She was as blind as a bat. What does the expression mean?		
He is sleeping like a baby. What does the expression mean?		
The moon is made of green cheese. What does the expression mean?		
The stars are like diamonds. What does the expression mean?		
I'm so hungry I could eat a horse. What does the expression mean?		
You are as strong as an ox. What does the expression mean?		
She is as tough as nails. What does the expression mean?		
That's not my cup of tea. What does the expression mean?		

Standards and Benchmarks: 1A, 1B, 1C, 1D, 1E, 1H, 2A, 2B, 2C, 2D, 3A, 3B, 3C, 3D, 3E, 3F, 3G, 3H, 3I, 3J, 3K, 3L

Figurative Language *(cont.)*

Bad Hair Day

When I woke up to the screeching of the alarm clock, I knew Monique had tampered with the buttons. Instead of a Top 40 tune, I got scritch-scratch static as loud as a freight train in a tunnel. So, after I picked my ears off the pillow and twisted them back into position, I shuffled like a snail into the hallway to wait my turn for the bathroom so I could get ready for school.

Leaning against the wall like a newspaper on a doorstep was my sinister sister, smiling mischievously. Then she blurted out, "Your hair! You look like crows have made a nest on your head."

I lunged; my hands were vulture's claws pushing her to the ground. My dad barreled out of the bathroom, shaving cream covering his face. And when he shouted, "Get off your sister!" a big blob of shaving cream slithered into his mouth, and the taste must have been awful because right then he turned into a chameleon—turning pale green, yellow, and pink.

Then, my dad looked at me and said, "Wow. Fix that mop, would you?"

"What mop?" I asked.

"On your head! Your hair looks like a tangle of thorns!"

I looked into the hall mirror, which stared back at me, silently taunting, "Nice hair! Hey, they might stick you in a monkey cage with hair like that!" I grabbed the hairbrush, but the thing seemed to tremble and bristle in terror as it neared my unruly mane, so I admitted defeat and sought assistance.

Dejectedly, I padded into my mom's bedroom.

"Help!" I pleaded.

When my mom turned, her eyes twinkled, but her voice sympathized, "Another bad hair day?"

"Yes." I sat on the edge of her bed as if waiting to get a shot at the doctor's.

Her slippers silently skittered under her bathrobe as she approached me, her hand holding a comb with its sharp teeth glinting as if to say, "The more knots the better!" My hair was a tangled rope on a sailing vessel, and I dreaded every second of my mom's combing. I felt at least a billion hairs being yanked from my scalp, and I knew I'd soon be bald.

But when I finally looked in the mirror, I was transformed. I was a knight who had conquered the dragon—with a little help from the queen!

Discussion Questions
- Identify all examples of figurative language.
- Identify the conflict in "Bad Hair Day."
- What is the theme in "Bad Hair Day?"

Writing Activity
Write about a haircut, hairstyle, good or bad "hair day" from your personal experience. Try to use one example from each of the six different figures of speech. Share with the class.

Standards and Benchmarks: 1A, 1B, 1C, 1D, 1E, 1I, 2A, 2B, 2C, 2D, 3A, 3B, 3C, 3D, 3E, 3F, 3G, 3H, 3I, 3J, 3K, 3L

Figurative Language *(cont.)*

Using Figurative Language

Describe a member of your family, using one example each from the following figures of speech: *simile, metaphor, personification, hyperbole, alliteration*, and *onomatopoeia*. Prior to writing, complete a character sketch of this family member.

Family Member

- simile: _____
- metaphor: _____
- personification: _____
- hyperbole: _____
- alliteration: _____
- onomatopoeia: _____

Now combine all the figures of speech into one paragraph. Use the back of this paper or a separate sheet, as your teacher directs. Share the paragraphs. Illustrate the figures of speech in the paragraph— that is, provide specific examples of the family member's action, speech, or behavior that demonstrate the figure of speech.

An Amazing Individual

Describe a person you find truly amazing by using figures of speech to show just how amazing this person is. With figurative language, this person should become larger than life!

A person I find amazing is _____

Three reasons I find this person amazing are:

1. _____
2. _____
3. _____

- simile: _____
- metaphor: _____
- personification: _____
- hyperbole: _____
- alliteration: _____
- onomatopoeia: _____

Combine your sentences into one narrative paragraph showing why this person is amazing. Illustrate the figurative language to accompany the paragraph.

Standards and Benchmarks: 1A, 1B, 1C, 1D, 1E, 1H, 2A, 2B, 2C, 2D, 3A, 3B, 3C, 3D, 3E, 3F, 3G, 3H, 3I, 3J, 3K, 3L

Sensory Imagery

Sensory imagery draws readers into narrative writing through the five senses.

For each place, use each of the five senses to describe the setting.

❑ **At a bakery,**

- I see_____
- I hear_____
- I taste_____
- I touch_____
- I smell_____

❑ **At a veterinarian's office,**

- I see_____
- I hear_____
- I taste_____
- I touch_____
- I smell_____

❑ **At a movie theater,**

- I see_____
- I hear_____
- I taste_____
- I touch_____
- I smell_____

❑ **At a science laboratory,**

- I see_____
- I hear_____
- I taste_____
- I touch_____
- I smell_____

Choose one of the above settings from which you have a personal memory. Cluster this memory in your journal. Write a one-paragraph narrative about your experience, inviting the reader to share in your memory through the use of sensory imagery. You should appeal to all five senses. Illustrate what you see, hear, taste, touch, and smell. Share your paragraphs.

52   ©2000 Teacher Created Materials, Inc.

 **Standards and Benchmarks:** 1A, 1B, 1C, 1D, 1E, 1H, 2A, 2B, 2C, 2D, 3A, 3B, 3C, 3D, 3E, 3F, 3G, 3H, 3I, 3J, 3K, 3L

Sensory Imagery *(cont.)*

Sold!

Imagine that you are a realtor and are selling your home. Write a description of your neighborhood, using appeals to the five senses. (Remember, you are trying to *sell* your home, not vacate it!)

Type of house: _____

Age of house: _____

Address: _____

Location: (near city, playgrounds, country, etc.) _____

At my house, I can . . .

see _____

hear _____

taste _____

touch_____

smell_____

Description of house: (how many rooms, bedrooms, garage, etc., including a picture or illustration) _____

Choose three rooms to describe in detail:

Room 1: _____

Room 2: _____

Room 3: _____

Describe the house and the surrounding area during each of the four seasons, using sensory imagery and figurative language.

Fall

_____

_____

_____

Winter

_____

_____

_____

Spring

_____

_____

_____

Summer

_____

_____

_____

Standards and Benchmarks: 1A, 1B, 1C, 1D, 1E, 1G, 2A, 2B, 2C, 2D, 3A, 3B, 3C, 3D, 3E, 3F, 3G, 3H, 3I, 3J, 3K, 3L

Sensory Imagery *(cont.)*

The First Time

Imagine that you are describing the following things to someone who has all five senses but has never smelled, heard, seen, touched, or tasted them. Use figurative language and sensory imagery to convey meaning. Choose one from each category to develop into a paragraph.

How would you describe the smell of the following things?

- apple pie
- ocean breeze
- freshly cut grass
- clean hair
- barbecue grill
- garbage
- popcorn

How would you describe the following sounds?

- baby's laugh
- fog horn
- package being unwrapped
- bacon cooking
- dog crying
- foreign accent
- radio static

How would you describe these images and objects?

- broken mirror
- city skyline

- orchard
- billboard
- ocean waves
- fast-food restaurant
- limousine

How would you describe touching these things?

- cooked pasta
- caterpillar
- computer keyboard
- a hairbrush
- window screen
- stuffed animal
- glass jar

How would you describe the taste of these things?

- French fries
- salad dressing
- stamps or envelope glue
- medicine
- salt water
- soap

Standards and Benchmarks: 1A, 1B, 1C, 1D, 1E, 1G, 1H, 2A, 2B, 2C, 2D, 3A, 3B, 3C, 3D, 3E, 3F, 3G, 3H, 3I, 3J, 3K, 3L

Tools for the Writing Process

Punctuating Conversation

When composing narratives, dialogue is often used to show how characters speak, as well as their exact words or responses to situations or questions. With research, you must use quotation marks when you use someone's exact words. You must also use quotation marks if you take information from another source (book, encyclopedia, Internet, newspaper, magazine) and present it as it appears in the actual text.

For each *rule*, students should practice writing dialogue by first brainstorming a possible narrative idea for the quotation and then writing a brief narrative based on the quotation. In the examples below, there is space under each rule and example for a practice sentence that uses the same pattern.

All sample quotations may also be used as journal ideas. Students should think of a personal incident similar to the quotation.

Students can also think of fiction narratives based on quotations.

1. **Quotation marks go around the exact words of a person.**

   "Sticks and stones may hurt my bones, but names? Sometimes they hurt the most," Sarah admitted.

   Practice Sentence: _____

   _____

   _____

2. **Periods, question marks, and commas go inside quotation marks (except under special circumstances) .**

   "That's crazy. You expect me to believe that?" Molly questioned, but looked out the window just the same.

   Practice Sentence: _____

   _____

   _____

3. **Commas set off quotations.**

   "Keep on dreaming," her mother whispered, "because sometimes dreams come true."

   Practice Sentence: _____

   _____

   _____

Tools for the Writing Process *(cont.)*

Punctuating Conversation *(cont.)*

4. When a quotation is divided, if the quote is one sentence, a comma is placed inside the first set of quotation marks, and another comma is used to set off the remainder of the sentence.

"And then," he paused dramatically and put his right hand over his heart, "she looked at me. Me! I swear it!"

Practice Sentence: _____

_____

5. When a quotation is divided, if the quote is one sentence, a comma is placed inside the first set of quotation marks, and another comma is used to set off the remainder of the sentence.

"I've seen a hot air balloon," Mr. Jensen declared. "But let me just tell ya, it didn't float in the sky. No sir, it floated right into my shop and if I had a pin—and if it was the kind of balloon ya could pop. Well, let's just say it would be a balloon no more"

Practice Sentence: _____

_____

6. When the speaker changes, begin the next quotation with a new paragraph.

"Daddy, are you awake?" Daniel pried his father's eyelids open.

"Um," his dad grunted, "but your mother is."

"Oh Daddy," Daniel cried, "Mommy said you were awake!"

Practice Sentence: _____

_____

7. When quoting material within context, put quotation marks around the words taken directly from the source.

"When she heard the poet say, 'Icicles are frozen tears, reminding us of life's sorrows,' she felt obligated to mention that icicles always melt. She raised her hand at the poem's conclusion, and when the poet began his next reading, she cleared her throat to get his attention.

Practice Sentence: _____

_____

8. If paraphrasing or conducting research and restating information in your own words, no quotation marks are necessary.

The poet fidgeted in his chair at the girl's comment, but regained composure and stated that an icicle, although beautiful, is sharp and cold, and that was his message in his poem "Frozen Fear."

Practice Sentence: _____

_____

Tools for the Writing Process *(cont.)*

Editing Marks

Editing is the last stage before rewriting a paper for publication. Careful attention is paid here to removing grammatical and spelling errors. Universal editing marks are valuable because the same mark in an English classroom in Maine means the same thing in Wisconsin, Texas, and Alaska. Of course, you may develop your own marks or styles for personal revisions. In peer revisions, however, it is important to use universal marks. Use the chart below as your guide to these universal editing and proofreading marks.

Editor's Mark	Meaning	Example
℮	Delete	It was was very tiny.
≡	Capitalize	the boy ran quickly.
/	Use lowercase	Many Athletes ran in the marathon.
∧	Insert a word	I want an ice cream sundae.
RO	Run-on sentence	Who's there what do you want?
frag.	Sentence fragment	Although the peddler's cart. frag
SP	Spelling error	Monkies swung in the trees.
∽	Reverse letters or words	Five books on were the shlef.
⊙	Add a period	Children played all day⊙
∧	Add a comma	I like apples peaches, and pears.
⌄	Add an apostrophe	John's puppy is cute.
⌄⌄ ⌄⌄	Add quotation marks	Help! cried.
¶	Begin a new paragraph	"Hello," said Carla. "Hi," Beth replied.
#	Make a space	I love Frenchfries.
⌒	Close the space	He lives in the country side.
stet	Do not delete (Let it stand.)	The beautiful swan flew away. stet

Revising

Ultimately, you are the boss of your writing. However, letting parents, teachers, friends, and classmates read your narratives will offer insights that perhaps you cannot see. Sometimes you know a narrative in your own head and can picture characters and settings, but maybe the narrative doesn't paint a clear picture for readers. Giving others the opportunity to review your narratives will enable you to discover whether others understood your narrative, enjoyed your narrative, and empathized with your characters or situation.

Tools for the Writing Process *(cont.)*

Self-Revision Checklist

❑ **Step 1**

Read your story aloud. Pause at commas and stop at periods. If you find yourself pausing, you may be missing a comma. (This is not a sure-fire test, of course, since commas are placed for grammatical reasons, not as breathing guides.) If you find yourself needing to stop, check to see if you have a run-on sentence or simply a sentence that is too long. Often your ear can "hear" mistakes. Maybe you have left out a word, or something just doesn't seem quite right. Instead of stopping the flow of the narrative, put an X in the margin. After you finish reading, go back and analyze the Xs that mark the spots!

❑ **Step 2**

List the parts of the story for proper sequencing of events.

• Beginning: _____

• Middle:_____

• Climax:_____

• End: _____

❑ **Step 3**

Check to see that all components of a successful narrative are included.

• **Conflict:** Is conflict presented in the beginning so the reader is intrigued? What is the conflict? How is the conflict resolved?

• **Characters:** Are the characters original or stereotypes? Can you identify or visualize the characters? Are the characters' personalities consistent with their actions?

• **Setting:** Can you imagine where the narrative takes place?

• **Flow:** Are there unnecessary scenes? Are there scenes which need to be added?

• **Dialogue:** Does the dialogue contribute to the story? Is the dialogue realistic?

❑ **Step 4**

Read the narrative for description. Identify examples of figurative language, sensory imagery, and strong verbs. Copy five examples of such phrases, sentences, or words in the space below and identify the type of description for each example.

a._____

b._____

c._____

d._____

e._____

❑ **Step 5**

Revise. Give to the group for reader-response suggestions.

❑ **Step 6**

Use reader-response comments for completing revisions.

❑ **Step 7**

Publish the final narrative.

Tools for the Writing Process *(cont.)*

Reader Response

It is important for a reader to express clear opinions so the writer will know what worked and what still needs work in the narrative.

When completing peer reader response check sheets, "yes" or "no" comments are worthless. If given the question, "Did you enjoy the narrative?" and you respond with either a yes or a no, what has the author learned? Nothing, except that it is possible you may not have read the narrative!

Use these pointers to review narratives constructively.

1. Identify the problem.

Be specific with your comments. Use examples from the story.

2. Consider feelings.

A statement such as, "What kind of loser would write a story like this?" is hurtful as well as unhelpful.

3. Speak for yourself.

Give your views only! Separate your personal views from your analysis of the writing. "I can't see why anyone would be interested in your narrative!" might instead be phrased, "I'm not really interested in basketball, but I understood the theme 'practice makes perfect.'"

4. Identify the good.

Be specific about what you like. "You described the setting so well and used such strong sensory imagery that I really felt I went on a horseback ride!"

5. Share your final reactions.

"I learned quite a bit on this topic, and I now want to become involved in the protection of animals. I won't purchase any more products that condone cruelty to animals." If you really weren't "moved" at all by the narrative, give reasons how the author could improve in order to make you more sympathetic.

Assessment Rubrics

The assessment rubrics follow the reader-response check sheets and should be examined so that you as students are aware of the assessment components. Assessment rubrics are valuable because you then become aware of the grading criteria and know what you need to do in order to receive a high mark on your narrative. Assessment rubrics are helpful to writing teachers because the grading is simplified and less time-consuming. They also help the teacher become an integral part in the drafting and revising portions of each student's narrative. When you and the teacher read the final portfolio piece, you will remember the changes that were recommended, note the revisions, and see the final transformation.

Personal Narratives

Personal narratives are true stories based upon the experiences of the author. As an author you may ask, "What is intriguing about me?" Well, people like to read true narratives because they can put themselves in the narrator's position and actually experience the story.

All personal narratives are written in the first person point of view. First person means using "I" as the narrator. If the narrative is written well, the reader may believe that he or she is "I" because the reader is thinking, "doing," and feeling what the narrator of the story is thinking, doing, and feeling.

In personal narratives, the reader wants to be invited to share in the story. If you are writing about a sad experience, the goal for you is to make your readers sad as well. If you are writing about a trip to the Grand Canyon, your readers (who may have never been to the Grand Canyon and may never have the opportunity to visit the Grand Canyon) should be able to see the Grand Canyon through your vivid descriptions and sensory imagery.

The beginning is the most essential part of the personal narrative. In the first paragraph, you have to grab your reader and make the reader want to read the story. The characters must be true-to-life, and presented so the reader can see them. Introducing the conflict is crucial. The reader will want to know how the characters deal with the conflict, so the experience of reading becomes not only enjoyable but also a learning experience. Readers will have the personal narrative to reflect upon if ever they find themselves in a similar circumstance or predicament.

Personal narratives have themes that help the reader to remember the narrative. Finishing the narrative, the reader will think—and come to his or her own understanding of the story. The theme may be somewhat different for the next reader, but what is important is that the narrative has given the readers something to take with them, to internalize, to process somewhere inside themselves.

Personal narratives are descriptive and detailed. Strong verbs, precise nouns, smooth transitions, figurative language, and sensory imagery all contribute to the strength of the narrative. The story that has become a part of you is now a part of others.

Each personal narrative writing activity contains prewriting activities to make the actual writing accessible. Along with the activities, the Prewriting Guide (page 61) may also be used to gather thoughts and ideas before beginning a personal narrative.

Standards and Benchmarks: 1A

Prewriting Guide

Topic of Narrative: _____

❑ **Getting Ideas**

• Relate personally to the topic: personal memories, real events, creative ideas.

• Cluster the topic: the first words that come to mind about the topic.

• Brainstorm any thoughts or feelings about this topic.

❑ **Identify the Story**

• Who:_____

• What: _____

• Where: _____

• When:_____

• Why:_____

• How:_____

❑ **Plot Jot**

• Ten Questions Related to the Plot Jot: (Use the back of this page for your answer.)

• Beginning: _____

• Middle:_____

• Climax:_____

• End: _____

❑ **Components of Narratives**

• Conflict(s): _____

• Characters (Use character sketch for more thorough analysis.):_____

• Setting: _____

• Theme: _____

• Point of View: _____

❑ **Sources for Information**

• _____

• _____

• _____

• _____

• _____

• _____

Standards and Benchmarks: 1A, 1B, 1C, 1D, 1E, 1H, 2A, 2B, 2C, 2D, 3A, 3B, 3C, 3D, 3E, 3F, 3G, 3H, 3I, 3J, 3K, 3L

What's in a Name?

Description

Research your name and write a personal narrative about your name and nicknames.

Prewriting Activities

- Write your full name at the top of a journal page.

- List who or what you were named for.

- List the nicknames given to you by family members, friends, teachers, and even yourself. List your nicknames from the past and any of your nicknames that have changed as you have grown. Tell why you were given these nicknames. You may need to ask parents and relatives about particular nicknames or nicknames given to you as a child.

- Research your name and what it means. Does this definition fit you? Give reasons to support your answer. Respond in your journal.

- If you could change your name or give yourself a nickname, what would the name be and why? Respond in your journal and discuss.

- What are some nicknames you have given your friends? Why do we give nicknames to other people? Respond in your journal and discuss.

Writing

Write a personal narrative about your name or one or more nicknames. You may choose to write how your nicknames have changed over the years, what nicknames mean to you, or if you feel content with the name you have been given. Incorporate the definition of your name in an appropriate place within your narrative.

Publishing

Bring in a baby picture of yourself. Have your teacher post class baby pictures on the bulletin board, with index cards identifying each picture as A, B, C, D, etc. Have classmates see who can correctly identify the most pictures, matching them to the personal narratives about names.

Technology Connection

Word-process the narratives. Use the Internet for researching names.

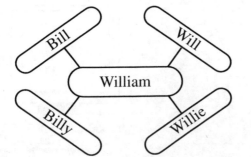

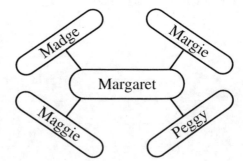

Standards and Benchmarks: 1A, 1B, 1C, 1D, 1E, 1H, 2A, 2B, 2C, 2D, 3A, 3B, 3C, 3D, 3E, 3F, 3G, 3H, 3I, 3J, 3K, 3L

Daydreaming

Description

Write a personal narrative about daydreaming.

Prewriting Activities

- Cluster the word "daydream" in your journals.
- Free-write a response to the question "If you were to daydream right at this moment, where would you go?" Share responses after an allotted time.

Discussion

- Why do we daydream?
- What are the benefits of daydreaming?
- Using the Comparison Graphic Organizer (page 136), compare daydreams to night dreaming.

Writing

Write a personal narrative about a time when you daydreamed. Describe the circumstances that led to your "letting go" and entering your daydream. Describe what your daydream gave you. Is daydreaming used as an escape? as a hope? to act out situations? Be sure to return to the "real world" and use transitions to keep the flow of narrative. What did the daydream succeed in doing?

Publishing

Create clouds out of white paper. Write your daydream on a cloud, using string to suspend it from the ceiling. Create a collage of your daydream on the second cloud and place it on a bulletin board with the title, "Where Do You Go When You Daydream?" Share the narratives with the class.

Technology Connection

Word-process the narrative. Italicize the "daydream" section. Take a picture or download a picture or image from the Internet that captures the image of your daydream. Create a slide show of images to share.

Where Do You Go When You Daydream?

 **Standards and Benchmarks:** 1A, 1B, 1C, 1D, 1E, 1H, 1L, 2A, 2B, 2C, 2D, 3A, 3B, 3C, 3D, 3E, 3F, 3G, 3H, 3I, 3J, 3K, 3L

Disappointing Others

Description
Write a personal narrative about a time you disappointed someone.

Prewriting Activities
- Brainstorm incidents when you disappointed your parents, relatives, a teacher, or a friend. Include the list in your personal journals for future topics.
- Choose one and free-write about the incident. Share.

Discussion
- How do you feel when you know you have disappointed someone? How does this person react?
- What do you do to remedy the situation?

Initiation

It was supposed to be a dream-come-true. A group of girls at Camp Columbia, the popular ones, of course, pull me into their cabin and ask me to be "one of them."

I dare ask myself, "Why?" After all, I'm neither ugly nor pretty but in that in-between-place of braces and pimples, hair that goes every way but the right way, and clothes that are either too tight or falling off. I'm not a brain, but I'm no dummy. I'm as close to average as you can get. Why would the most popular girls at camp seek me out to become one of them? Remember, I'm no dummy.

The girls—I don't even know their names; they all look and act like identical octuplets—go on and on about how beautiful, smart, fun, and adventurous I am. "Me?" I think to myself, "Wow, they must really like me!" That voice exclaiming, "Warning! Danger!" is crunched because these are words that average people like me never hear.

Each girl takes a turn buttering me up, but I never stop to think this couldn't possibly be true, because these are words I've never heard before. And then the jelly is slapped on, and the girls tell me what an asset I'd be to their "club."

The voice tries to sneak out, but I ignore it. I've always wanted to be wanted, to be accepted, to be liked and admired, to be popular—just like these eight girls.

"So, will you join us?" the leader (I assume) asks.

"Yes." I don't even hesitate. "Should I let my counselor know I'll sleep over here from now on? Let me go pack my sleeping bag!"

Giggles should warn me, but I take them as giggles of happiness.

"Well, first, you have to pass the test." One of the girls pulls out a clipboard with a list of questions. I want to mention, "You just listed 18 things about me that are so wonderful, why do I have to take a test?" But I refrain. How difficult could the test be?

"Okay," a tall girl settles into her bunk, "Question one. Who is Letitia?"

"She's my best friend," I answer confidently.

"Really?" someone murmurs, and the others echo.

Disappointing Others *(cont.)*

Initiation *(cont.)*

"Yeah, uh-huh, why?" The back of my neck itches, and my sandals feel slippery.

"Well, she isn't exactly," the next part is whispered, "one of us."

"Oh." I feel like my chance at being the new "My Fair Lady" has just been ruined. I wish I had never been invited or accepted the invitation to Cabin 12.

"So, you really like Letitia?" one girl asks. All of their voices are so similar, I can't even distinguish who asked me the question.

"Yeah, I mean, sure," I mutter. "Sometimes."

"So, she isn't really your best friend?" the collective group of girls question.

"No, I mean. No. I guess not." I choke out my words.

Suddenly, Letitia throws off a sleeping bag and jumps down from the top bunk. I feel emptiness inside, and my heart and mind spin uncontrollably. My eyes fill with fear and sadness at the loneliness enveloping me.

Letitia stumbles out of the cabin, amidst laughter and cries of, "Did you see her face?" I wonder if they are talking about mine or Letitia's. It really doesn't matter.

I remain, feet rooted to the floor, until someone says, "Well?"

My silence creates a stillness never known at Camp Columbia until now.

I meet eight pairs of eyes with a look I can't even explain. But I'm sure it's a look they will always remember, for I penetrate deep into the souls of each girl with that voice that wanted to tell me what to do. Somehow, I find myself exiting Cabin 12 and running up the dirt path to Cabin 3, where I hope to fix what is now broken.

Discussion

- Discuss as a class whether the relationship/friendship can be mended.
- Discuss why the narrator acted the way she did. Discuss the power of peer pressure.

Writing

- From the point of view of the narrator, write about the next meeting with Letitia.
- Write about a time you disappointed parents or a friend. Incorporate parents' or friends' reactions and tell how the situation was resolved.

Publishing

Share the narrative with parents and ask them to write their reactions to the narrative on an index card. Share these with the class if you choose.

Technology Connection

Word-process the narrative. Create a flow chart depicting your action and reaction. Choose symbols to represent individuals. For example, you may be represented by a square, your parents may be represented by a circle, and the reactions may be in the shape of diamonds, with arrows showing the various sources.

Standards and Benchmarks: 1A, 1B, 1C, 1D, 1E, 1H, 2A, 2B, 2C, 2D, 3A, 3B, 3C, 3D, 3E, 3F, 3G, 3H, 3I, 3J, 3K, 3L

A Good Friend

Description

Write a personal narrative about when you realized the importance of friendship.

Prewriting Activities

- Cluster the word "friend" in your journals.
- From the cluster, students should write one paragraph on their definition of a good friend. Share the paragraphs.
- On the chalkboard, brainstorm a list of traits that a good friend needs.
- In your journal free-write a response to this question: Is it better to have one best friend or a handful of friends? Why? Share journal responses.
- Initiate class discussion on whether friends have to be your own age, if friends can also be relatives, and why friendships end.

Writing

Write a personal narrative about a time when you realized just how important friends are. It may be a time when you needed a friend and didn't have one, when you were a good friend to someone, or when someone was a good friend to you.

Publishing

Share the friend narratives.

Technology Connection

Word-process the narrative. Create a pie chart showing the characteristics of your good friend. Weigh the characteristics that you feel are the most important in your chart.

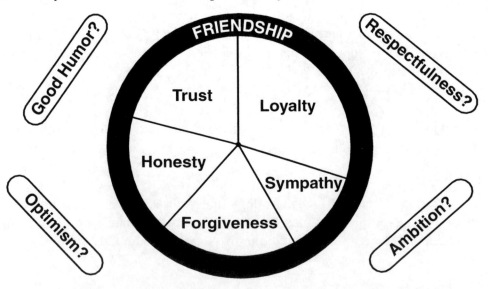

Standards and Benchmarks: 1A, 1B, 1C, 1D, 1E, 1H, 1L, 2A, 2B, 2C, 2D, 3A, 3B, 3C, 3D, 3E, 3F, 3G, 3H, 3I, 3J, 3K, 3L

I'll Always Remember

Description

Compose a narrative letter to a grandparent, sharing an important memory.

The Admiral

We peeled ourselves out of the station wagon, the vinyl imprinted on the backs of our legs, and stretched. Finally, we were at my grandmother's new house, only minutes away from Mickey Mouse!

"You're here to meet your new grandfather," our parents reminded us, as my brothers and I noticed the oranges in the trees lining the driveway, the lemons and limes in bushel baskets near the front door, and grapefruits dangling like softballs.

My grandmother met us at the front door, as did my new grandfather. As I waited my turn for hugs and kisses, I analyzed my new granddad. He didn't look new. He looked old, just like a granddad should. When he hugged me, he tousled my hair, and his arms were strong, and he didn't want to let me go. Plus, he whispered, "I bet you can't wait to go to the Magic Kingdom!" He knew the real reason we had driven for nearly three days.

I smiled. The only thing new about my granddad was the house. I didn't remember where we were to sleep or the fancy chandelier over the dining room table. I didn't remember the medals shining behind glass, the camel saddle, or the ivory statues hiding in the ferns. I didn't remember the brick path that led to a private backyard beach nor the boat docked in the lake.

But soon, I remembered the house and more. How many times my grandfather sat in the lake with me, holding my tips up while I learned to water ski, and later as he sat in the window while I slalomed around the lake. How many times he told our favorite stories over and over, about Annapolis, the war, the Purple Heart, and later when I brought him joy telling him my stories.

My granddad was never "new" to me. But he did give me new memories which I will cherish forever, every year I visited his house on the lake, with the lemon trees, the white sand beach, and yes, Mickey Mouse. Most of all I remember my granddad's love and generosity. Because once upon a time, long, long ago, I was new to him. And he treated his new granddaughter as if we had always been together.

Discussion

Describe the relationship between the grandfather and the granddaughter.

Writing

Write a letter to a grandparent retelling a memory you hold dear.

Technology Connection

Scan a recent photograph of yourself for grandparents to download from an e-mail letter if they have an e-mail address. If not, word-process and use a large font (if that is easier for your grandparent or relative to read). Use colors or different styles to add emphasis.

Standards and Benchmarks: 1A, 1B, 1C, 1D, 1E, 1H, 1L, 2A, 2B, 2C, 2D, 3A, 3B, 3C, 3D, 3E, 3F, 3G, 3H, 3I, 3J, 3K, 3L

First Impressions

Description

Write about a time when your first impression of a person, place, or thing turned out to be incorrect.

Prewriting Activities

- Think of a person you know, about whom your first impression was wrong, for this person turned out to be quite the opposite. Free-write about this person. Include reflections upon your first meeting and the events that led you to change your mind.
- Think of a place you initially thought was one thing and soon discovered it was really not what it appeared to be. Free-write about this place. Include first impressions and why your opinions changed.
- Think of an object (possibly a gift or personal purchase) you initially thought was one thing but which turned out to be another. Free-write about this experience.
- Share three free-writes with the class.

The Bird Feeder

It was a class trip, and I had to go. Otherwise, you'd never catch me hiking through the woods swatting mosquitoes and belting black flies while attempting to "record nature" in my journal. All I've recorded are the welts the size of jelly beans on my legs and arms, despite the gallons of bug repellent I bathed in before the "Nature Hike."

Three days in the wilderness (the correct term is "our environment") without electricity! Portable radios weren't allowed. No one ever mentioned that we didn't even need shampoo. The bathhouse consists of three toilets and a sink large enough for Smokey the Bear.

The boys' and girls' camps are separated by the dining hall and miles of snake-infested terrain. As if we'd dare sneak to the boys' side guided only by a flashlight, which was allowed. I'll make a note in my journal that after a five-mile hike, bug repellent masks body odor.

On the first day we had mandatory activities: orienteering, fire building, plant identification, first aid, and shelter-building. Camping in my backyard is the closest I'll ever get to camping again. No need to know how to construct a branch and twig shelter there. On the second day we could pick our own activities—like "Mountain Biking," "Celebrate Thoreau," "Bog Jog," and "Trash and Treasures." I chose "Bird Watching." I figured it would include a nice hike, even better resting spot, and a pair of binoculars. Boy, was I wrong!

First Impressions *(cont.)*

The Bird Feeder *(cont.)*

A five-mile hike left me with barely a squeeze of hydrocortisone cream, and ducking the underbrush had my hair follicles crying for soap. The ascent burned my thighs, and my hamstrings ached. P.E. was easy compared to this. When we reached the top, I forgot about my itching and hamburger craving, for we had reached the top of the world. We were on a cliff of white quartz, streaked with silver, and we actually looked down on the pine trees. The clouds were touchable, and I had never been so close to the sun or felt the blue of a sky like that.

I thought a bird was a bird, but again I was wrong. We identified, first by sound, cedar waxwings and ovenbirds. We located turkey vultures, blue birds, warblers, and woodpeckers. And even though I had seen chickadees and goldfinches at our bird feeder, they, along with the sparrows and cardinals, never looked more beautiful than in their natural environment.

My journal was full of sketches, information, and . . . poems. Me! I've never been inspired to write a poem, let alone share it with a group on the top of the world! Our descent was too quick. We talked about the differences among birds—from the songs they sang to their appearance. At the bath house I recognized an ovenbird, "Chip-chip, chip!" Because I tried to locate him, I didn't have time to dunk my head and shampoo, for the dinner horn blared angrily.

But the following morning, the horn from the bus was much more disturbing.

Discussion

- Describe the changes the main character goes through.
- Free-write on the phrase "Don't judge a book by its cover," and then share the thoughts in discussion.

Writing

Write about a person, place, or thing where your first impression turned out to be exactly the opposite of what you originally thought. Include the situation which provided your first impression and the circumstances that changed your mind.

Publishing

Place narratives on a bulletin board with the heading "Don't Judge a Book by Its Cover." Share the narratives.

Technology Connection

Word-process the narratives. Create a computer illustration or edit an existing image for the cover page. The cover should capture your first impression. At the end of the narrative, a new picture should be used that captures your new impression.

Standards and Benchmarks: 1A, 1B, 1C, 1D, 1E, 1G, 1H, 2A, 2B, 2C, 2D, 3A, 3B, 3C, 3D, 3E, 3F, 3G, 3H, 3I, 3J, 3K, 3L

Every Day Brings a Story

Description

Write a personal narrative about a specific time frame.

Prewriting Activities

- Keep a time log over three consecutive days. Details should be written for every half-hour. Begin at 6:00 A.M., and continue at 6:30, 7:00, 7:30, etc. The goal is to be specific and include details.

Sample Log

6:30 P.M. Ate dinner late because the self-timer didn't turn on. Instead of having meatloaf, we ordered a pizza. I'm relieved the self-timer didn't work. Mom, Dad, and I finished off a whole pepperoni pie. Nellie, the dog, got the crusts. Mom and Dad talked about politics. I could care less about politics, so I just ate. It's my turn to do dishes on Wednesday night, and cleanup was a breeze. I threw the paper plates and the box in the dumpster outside our building. Then I was told I had to take Nellie out. And let me tell you, after a dog eats pepperoni pizza crusts, well, maybe meatloaf would have been better!

- Include any dreams you may remember from sleeping time—guess on the time!
- Bring the completed time log to your group. Group members will read the log and highlight a three-to five-hour time block which they found not only most intriguing, but also a period they would like more details about.
- This highlighted section will be the basis of your personal narrative.

Writing

- Using the time frame selected by your group, create a personal narrative.
- If you feel another time frame is more interesting, explain to your group. They need to give you the okay. Persuasion is key!

Publishing

- Place the narratives on a bulletin board with the heading "Every Day Brings a Story!"
- Illustrate your narratives in comic strip style.

Technology Connection

- Word-process the narratives.
- E-mail your latest story to a friend or relative.

 **Standards and Benchmarks:** 1A, 1B, 1C, 1D, 1E, 1G, 1H, 1L, 2A, 2B, 2C, 2D, 3A, 3B, 3C, 3D, 3E, 3F, 3G, 3H, 3I, 3J, 3K, 3L

Things I Was Told

Description

Write about something you believed as a child but now, looking back, know it isn't true.

Prewriting Activities

As a class, generate a list of things you were told as children that you know are not true. For example:

- If you lie, your nose will grow.
- If you stick your arm out a window and you pass a telephone pole, your arm will fall off.
- If you aren't good, then Santa Claus won't come.
- If you don't eat your peas, you'll never grow.
- If you swallow a watermelon seed, a watermelon will grow from your belly button.
- If you don't wash behind your ears, potatoes will grow there.

Discussion

- Why do parents or others tell us things that are false? Is this wrong?
- After free-writing about something once believed as a child—this can be either something someone said or something made up on your own, like a monster under your bed—share the free-writes.

The Lollipop Tree

Nothing. Two weeks and still no green sprout stretched from the earth. Not even a glimpse of a white stick, or the arch of purple, green, yellow, or orange. None of my lollipops were growing. But next to my garden plot were my brother's sunflowers—planted on the same day at the same time of day, and they were already the size of a newly sharpened pencil.

Nevertheless, I filled the watering can, put in three shakes of "Magic Grow" crystals, and watered my lollipops. Warm days, a day or two of rain, and nothing popped from the soil. Yet the sunflowers were the size of Jack's beanstalk!

My brother joined me in the afternoon and mentioned, "Maybe they aren't growing 'cause you left the plastic on." He slurped his chocolate milk and added, "When I grew lollipops when I was your age, I took the plastic off."

When he left, I scooped through the dirt like a backhoe. All four lollipops emerged, along with dirt and one wriggly worm. I ripped off the plastic and neatly poked four holes in my garden, just the right size for my four lollipops. What wasted time!

Uncle Jimmy and Aunt Linda barbecued with us that night. They were so impressed with my brother's sunflowers, I couldn't wait to tell them about my garden.

"Uncle Jimmy, Aunt Linda—look! Soon we'll have all the lollipops in the world! Orange, grape, lime, and cherry, oh, I mean lemon. I think." I paused, trying to remember what flavors I had actually planted. I shrugged my shoulders and added, "Whatever the flavors, you can have as many as you want."

Things I Was Told *(cont.)*

The Lollipop Tree *(cont.)*

Uncle Jimmy and Aunt Linda smiled, in between bites of potato salad and baked beans. Then they burst out laughing and covered their mouths to keep the food from spilling out. My father choked on his hamburger, and my mother glared at my brother, who ate pickle after pickle.

"What's so funny?" I asked. "Craig said his lollipop tree had so many lollipops the candy store went out of business!"

"Sweetie," my mom held up her hand, motioning me to stop.

Craig looked at my uncle. "You should have seen her face when I told her you had to take the plastic off first!" And everyone roared this time, even my mother.

I barely ate any food and found it difficult to keep my eyes off my garden, where I had envisioned my lollipop trees growing, and now knew they never would.

But in my sleep that night, I smiled. For in my dreams, there will always be a place where lollipop trees grow and a pot of gold waits at the end of the rainbow.

Discussion

- What is the theme of "The Lollipop Tree"?
- Share in discussion of free-writing about a dream you wish would come true.
- Write the conversation between the narrator and Craig leading up to the planting of the lollipops. Read and discuss.

Writing

- Choose one thing someone told you or one thing you believed as a child. Write your narrative as a diary entry from the voice of a child. Share your feelings and concern about what you were told or about what you believed in. Describe the circumstance that led you to be given this information (that is, were you sticking your arms out of a moving vehicle?) or what led you to believe the thing under your bed existed (when you couldn't fall asleep, the noises and creak under your bed convinced you something else couldn't sleep as well). Be consistent in using the voice of a child!
- Next, write a diary entry about the same event, but as the person you are now. Reflect on the incident with new eyes.

Publishing

- Share diary entries with the class.
- Draw a picture of the "thing" you believed as a child or illustrate the concept of what someone told you.

Technology Connection

Word-process the narratives. Experiment with fonts for two diary entries. Use clip art or other computer images and create a child's book approximately eight to ten pages in length.

Standards and Benchmarks: 1A, 1B, 1C, 1D, 1E, 1G, 1H, 1L, 2A, 2B, 2C, 2D, 3A, 3B, 3C, 3D, 3E, 3F, 3G, 3H, 3I, 3J, 3K, 3L

Lucky

Description

Write a narrative sharing why you are lucky.

Prewriting Activities

In journals, you write about what being "lucky" means. In this entry, consider whether you are or are not lucky. Share your responses.

The Winning Ticket

I always do homework at the kitchen counter. The warm hum of the dishwasher drowns out the clutter of the day, so I can concentrate. But tonight I stare at my paper. Empty, endless, and blank. Just like my ideas. Our assignment in language arts is to write why we are lucky, and all day I was bothered because I am not lucky. I've never felt lucky, and I can't think of anything that makes me lucky. It's not that I don't have luck. It's just that I'm just like a person in an assembly line who plods along without anything exciting, good or bad, happening.

Oh, I could write about how my friends are lucky. Miguel is lucky because his brother drives him to school and home again in a red Mustang. He revs up the engine like he's about to take off in the Indy 500 before spinning out of the school parking lot. Now that is lucky. And Abby visits her father on weekends and always comes to school on Monday with some sort of trinket that everyone wants. That is lucky.

With no luck—see, this confirms it—I go into the living room where a glamorous game-show wannabe in her sequins and baubles and plastic smile gestures as each Powerball number flies to its final destination. Ha! No winners. No luck.

A powerful drum roll introduces "Eyewitness Nightly News." Top stories reveal: Hurricane threatens the South—evacuation planned for thousands! Traffic Advisory—Tractor-trailer jackknifes, interstate closed, at least three believed dead! Contaminated drinking water leaves inhabitants of a third-world community literally dying of thirst—Refugees return home, but to devastation. Their entire lives must be rebuilt!

Bad luck everywhere.

Lucky *(cont.)*

The Winning Ticket *(cont.)*

The next morning, while walking to school, I see a sign for two lost cats. I stop to admire the picture. Two pairs of yellow eyes shine amidst gray fur. Some kid's probably bawling, waiting for their return.

A couple blocks down another sign states "Moving Sale." Wow. I couldn't imagine living anywhere but here. I'd have to make new friends, leave my neighborhood, the arcade down the block, and the best pepperoni pizza in the country.

An ambulance screams by, a man in a wheelchair maneuvers onto the curb. Proof all around that luck is fictitious.

At school, I am surrounded by friends in the cafeteria. I crunch an apple picked on my family apple-picking expedition last weekend, and the sweet juice dribbles down my chin. Laughter hugs me tightly. An upcoming dance inspires my friends. Our win over Kingston empowers them. Their only concern is the science test next period.

I look forward to language arts because now I have plenty of ideas. How lucky is that?

Discussion

- Scan the headlines of a newspaper and note all the "news" and then write two columns on your paper, titled "Good News" and "Bad News." Share your results with the class in discussion.
- Free-write about a gift you received that cannot be touched or held but can be kept forever—love, a hug, kind words, good deed, help studying, words of encouragement, etc. Include who gave you this gift and why it is meaningful. Share responses in discussion.

Writing

Students should write a personal narrative about why they are lucky or unlucky and how they came to understand that they are, indeed, lucky or unlucky.

Publishing

Bring in a gift, if tangible, unless it is too sentimental or too valuable. Share your narrative with the person who gave you the gift.

Technology Connections

- Word-process the narrative.
- Create a cover with borders and experiment with font, size, and color. The cover should, in some appropriate way, reflect the gift.

Standards and Benchmarks: 1A, 1B, 1C, 1D, 1E, 1G, 1H, 1L, 2A, 2B, 2C, 2D, 3A, 3B, 3C, 3D, 3E, 3F, 3G, 3H, 3I, 3J, 3K, 3L

Pride

Description

Write a narrative about a time they were proud of themselves or others were proud of them.

Prewriting Activities

- Write "Achievement" in the middle of a journal page. Cluster.

- Define achievement on the chalkboard.

- Brainstorm a list of all of your achievements. You must have 10 achievements on your list! Discuss how achievements can be big or small—for example, how you never gossip, won the chess tournament, help take care of younger siblings, volunteer at the local soup kitchen, or play the piano.

- Ask parents about a time they were proud of you. Create a plot jot about this time and share it with the class.

- In journals, respond to the following questions: How did your parents' story about being proud of you make you feel? Do you remember the incident? Did you think they were going to write about that time, or a different time?

- Think of a time when you were most proud of yourself. Create a plot jot. With a group, come up with 10 questions about the plot jot. Answer the questions.

Last One In Is A Rotten Egg

If you've never been the last one picked for kickball, then you can stop reading. Then again, you may want to know that we kids realize if it was not for the gym teacher, we wouldn't be chosen at all. What you need to understand is that we don't really want to play kickball, and it doesn't matter that we are chosen last. We'd much rather finish the last chapter in our novel, or crack the last phase of our video game. It's not that we aren't athletic. We would simply prefer doing something else. And everyone has had that feeling. Even you.

But since physical education is a subject (and graded) we play kickball and run to the outfield, making sure we're next to the kids who yell, "I got it!"

We take our turn kicking when it's our turn, and even get on base twice. Then the whistle pierces through the air, and the gym teacher yells that you, "Yes, you!" are the new first baseman.

Suddenly, you have to be attentive. No longer can you waffle about nothing in the outfield. No longer can you sit on the bench bemoaning your turn. You must watch the game.

Pride *(cont.)*

Last One In Is A Rotten Egg *(cont.)*

Watch the—Thunk! The red sphere rockets to . . . the pitcher! The pitcher grabs the ball effortlessly and hurls it to you. Thunk. "Out!" yell your teammates and the teacher. Meanwhile, you find it difficult to breathe, but the next kicker is up, and you have to concentr—Thunk! The second baseman catches the ball. "Out!" you hear yourself shout with your team. You want to throw up, and you pray for an easy out. Kickball is now one notch lower—right behind clipping toenails, on your least-favorite-things-to-do list. But, like toenails, sometimes you don't have a choice.

Thunk! The rocket zooms miles above you, yet you leap into the heavens, fingertips touch and struggle to hold—hold—hold, yes! The ball is saved from exiting the galaxy. "Out!" the coach exclaims.

Your teammates are as shocked as you—their mouths hang open, their eyes stare at you in disbelief.

The game eventually ends. You need to change your T-shirt and probably your socks, too. Yet, everyone (on both teams) pats you on the back and says, "You played a great game."

When you look in the locker room mirror, you see that the secret is out. You can play. You can play kickball and you will no longer be the last person chosen. Somewhere inside, you feel good. You still don't like kickball, and you still want to finish your book, but from now on, sitting on the sidelines will be left for the others who are not willing to try.

Discussion

- What is the theme of "Last One In Is A Rotten Egg"?
- Write about the next physical education class when kickball is played. Use the point of view of the narrator or another classmate and share the writing in discussion.
- Identify all figurative language and discuss how it enhances the narrative.

Writing

Write about a proud moment in your life. Be sure to include some type of conflict to make your proud moment an even greater achievement!

Publishing

Design a medal to give yourself. Have it relate to your narrative. Have a class award ceremony. Give yourselves a standing ovation! Share narratives.

Technology Connections

- Word-process the narrative.
- Using a graphics program, create a medal and "Pride" award certificate.
- Have an award ceremony and display your medals and certificates.

76 ©2000 Teacher Created Materials, Inc.

Standards and Benchmarks: 1B, 1C, 1D, 2A, 2B, 2C, 2D, 3A, 3B, 3C, 3D, 3E, 3F, 3G, 3H, 3I, 3J, 3K, 3L

Reader Response Check Sheet

1. Does the narrative evoke empathy?_____

   Did you imagine yourself in the narrative?_____

   Could you feel what the main character felt?_____

   What was your emotional state at the end of the narrative?_____

   What was the theme?_____

   Give an example from the narrative to support the theme._____

   _____

2. Is the plot in sequential order?_____

   Is it logical?_____

   Identify the parts of the story.

      Beginning:_____

      Middle: _____

      Climax: _____

      End:_____

3. Which characters seem real?_____

   What is it about the characters which makes them believable? _____

4. Is the setting (time and place) well described or implied?_____

5. Is the conflict introduced at the beginning of the narrative? _____

   What is the conflict, the type of conflict, and how is the conflict resolved?_____

6. Is the dialogue realistic?_____

   Does dialogue enhance the narrative? _____

   What do you learn from the dialogue?_____

   If there is no dialogue, would the inclusion of dialogue benefit the narrative? _____

7. What was your first impression of the title? _____

   How does the title relate to the narrative? _____

8. How were you "hooked" from the first paragraph of the narrative? _____

9. Figurative Language Examples: _____

   Sensory Imagery Examples: _____

   Action Verbs: _____

10. Spelling/Punctuation: _____

11. What would you do to revise this narrative? _____

12. List three strengths of the narrative:_____

Assessment Rubric

The rubric is weighted at 100%. Ten is the highest single rating. Add up numbers to get a total score.

1. All prewriting activities were completed. 10 9 8 7 6 5 4 3 2 1 0	
2. During revision process, narrative shows not only revision but also incorporation of reader response comments. 10 9 8 7 6 5 4 3 2 1 0	
3. The theme is clear without being stated. 10 9 8 7 6 5 4 3 2 1 0	
4. The first paragraph/part of the narrative is intriguing, draws the reader in, and presents the conflict. 10 9 8 7 6 5 4 3 2 1 0	
5. The characters are lively, realistic, and their descriptions are true to their action. 10 9 8 7 6 5 4 3 2 1 0	
6. The setting is clear and described so the reader can visualize it. 10 9 8 7 6 5 4 3 2 1 0	
7. All parts of a story (beginning, middle, climax, and end) follow sequentially. The conflict is resolved. 10 9 8 7 6 5 4 3 2 1 0	
8. Figurative language, sensory imagery, and strong action verbs contribute to the story. 10 9 8 7 6 5 4 3 2 1 0	
9. Spelling and punctuation are correct. 10 9 8 7 6 5 4 3 2 1 0	
10. The overall presentation of the narrative is word-processed and published according to directions. 10 9 8 7 6 5 4 3 2 1 0	
Total Score	

Standards and Benchmarks: 1A, 4A, 4B, 4C, 4D, 4E, 4F, 4G, 4H

Techniques for Nonfiction Narratives

Nonfiction narratives contain all the elements of narrative writing: characters, setting, conflict, theme, and an engaging story line (plot) which invites the reader to become involved in the story. The nonfiction narrative is often written from the third person point of view. So that the nonfiction narrative does not become a mere "encyclopedic reading," figurative language, sensory imagery, and vivid description make the text come alive. Research is often needed for accuracy of information. Proper documentation is needed to show readers where information was obtained, and referencing sources within the narrative adds strength and credibility to your narrative.

Finding a Good Subject

Brainstorm people and topics interesting to you. Chances are, if you are interested in something or someone, then you already know something about your topic. In addition, you will present the narrative in a style that is intriguing to your readers. If you choose a subject which you don't find particularly interesting, gathering information will be cumbersome. When you are excited about a topic, research is viewed more like a scavenger hunt!

Brainstorm occupations or roles—"people types." For the following occupations and roles, name people whom you either know or find intriguing. Include a favorite and least favorite person in each category and write two reasons to support your opinion. As a class, brainstorm other occupations to include in the list. Then, from within those occupations, think of individuals whom you know or find intriguing.

Keep a list in your writing notebook for topics. Share your list with the class.

- relative
- musician
- store owner
- author
- athlete
- television personality
- neighbor
- friend
- hero
- criminal
- actor
- role model
- artist
- business leader
- environmentalist
- religious leader
- inventor
- teacher
- comedian
- politician
- historical figure

Identifying a Story

In order to be interesting, a nonfiction narrative needs *conflict*. If those we admire didn't struggle to achieve their dreams, their stories wouldn't be so interesting. The characters need to be presented accurately so we can visualize these people, so they seem real—with real human traits. When gathering information, note any conflicts. Research how these conflicts were resolved. Identifying conflict is the key to identifying a story.

Techniques for Nonfiction Narratives *(cont.)*

Gathering Information

Gathering information about a subject makes you more knowledgeable. When facts are incorporated into your narrative, the reader will believe what you say to be true. Also, the reader will see that you care about your subject and spent time researching material.

Ways to Gather Information

- Go directly to the source.
- Use information you already know.
- Read books.
- Research encyclopedias.
- Check the Internet.
- Ask friends.

- Ask relatives.
- Involve parents.
- Watch television programs.
- Read newspapers.
- Read magazines.

School library and computer/media specialists can assist in the demonstration of techniques for gathering information. Use their talents and knowledge to help you use specific equipment and resources.

Remember to note where information came from, so the sources will be correctly listed in a bibliography. Also, in case more information is needed, students will then know where to look for it.

Information Needed for Sources

- Book: author, title, city of publication, publisher, and date of publication
- Television Show: title of program, title of particular episode, date of program, channel, time of program
- Internet: title of site, date the site was last updated, author of site, Internet address, page number
- Magazine: magazine name, title of article, date of the magazine, author, pages of article
- Encyclopedia: name of encyclopedia, year published, volume number, page number, title of article

Note: Underline or italicize titles.

Bibliographic Format

Book: author, *title*. city, publisher, date.

Magazine: author, "article title." *magazine*, date of magazine, pages of article.

Encyclopedia: "heading of entry." *name of encyclopedia*. volume #, date, page numbers.

On-line Source: author of site, "title of Web site" [on-line]. (date of visit), Internet address, pages of Web site utilized.

Television: "title of program." date and time of program, channel.

Interview: name of interviewee. date, time, and place of interview.

Newspaper: author, "title of article." *newspaper name*, date of newspaper, pages of article.

 **Standards and Benchmarks:** 1A, 1B, 3A, 3B, 3C, 3D, 3E, 3F, 3G, 3H, 3I, 3J, 3K, 3L, 4A, 4B, 4C, 4D, 4E, 4F, 4G, 4H

Techniques for Nonfiction Narratives *(cont.)*

Activity

Work in groups, each group will be assigned a different topic, appropriately designated by the teacher. Ideas may include figures or incidents previously studied in the curriculum.

Your groups must find 10 facts from a variety of sources about the topic. Complete as much of a character sketch as you can. Identify a narrative about your topic by locating conflict. From the researched material, answer *who, what, where, when, why,* and *how* about the topic. Present your findings to the class.

Taking Notes

When information is located that may be useful in your nonfiction narrative, it is time to take notes. Taking notes helps you sort and remember information. There are two methods for taking notes: *paraphrasing* and *copying*. Paraphrasing is restating a passage in your own words. However, you must give credit to the source even when paraphrasing, as the material was really from someone else.

Copying is writing information down word for word. Material copied must be in quotation marks. Why? So the reader knows that the information came from a source and voice other than your own.

Not giving the source credit when copying directly is called *plagiarism*. Plagiarism is essentially stealing the words of another and calling them your own. Plagiarism is wrong and against the law!

Activity

Read a sample nonfiction narrative and practice paraphrasing the entire narrative or excerpts from the narrative. (An example of paraphrasing appears below.) Next, you will receive five follow-up questions based on the sample nonfiction narrative. Copy the answers directly from the narrative, maintaining the proper use of quotation marks. (Note the example of quoted material.)

Referencing Within a Narrative

When you write nonfiction narratives, often you reference people or sources directly in the narrative. So that the pace of the narrative will not be brought to a screeching halt, it is important to maintain the flow with little disruption. Footnotes are a way to properly reference information without disrupting the flow. (A footnote example is provided below.)

Direct Quotation Example

Naturalist author Jack Denton Scott believes that when you write nonfiction, you need to research "so that you will know perhaps more than you or anyone else will want to know."

Paraphrased Example

Jack Denton Scott, naturalist author, believes that researching is the key to writing successful nonfiction.

Footnote Example

The key to writing nonfiction is thorough research so that you know more than anyone else.[1]

[1] Scott, Jack, p. 7.

Standards and Benchmarks: 4A

Techniques for Nonfiction Narratives *(cont.)*

Interviewing

Before conducting an interview, you should gather information about the person or topic so that you have some knowledge, as well as a basis for formulating interview questions. You may discover some questions about the person or topic that you want answers to. You may want to answer *who, what, where, when, why,* and *how* as a brainstorming technique before creating questions. Complete a character sketch on the person whom you are interviewing. Star any missing information you feel might be essential to a successful interview. Check any information you would like more details for, or need to check for accuracy. The character sketch is a guide to making the interviewee seem real to your readers. By no means, however, should all the information be included in the narrative!

Guidelines for Successful Interviewing

1. **Contact the person to be interviewed.** Make an appointment. Allow at least one hour for the interview. One hour will ideally give you 45 minutes of valuable time. Inform the interviewee what your purpose is in conducting the interview (although this may change). By informing the person about your purpose, he or she may be able to bring material to share or give you and be "thinking" about information you may find interesting. In short, your interviewee will be prepared, just as you will be! You may ask this person if he or she would mind you tape recording the interview so that you don't lose time writing down answers and possibly missing information.

2. **Formulate questions.** When designing questions, ask yourself why you would like to know the answer. If you can't think of an answer, maybe the question is not worth asking. Don't hold your interview questions as unchangeable—you may think of new questions during your interview. Your interview may lead you down a new path. If this path is interesting, then pursue it. If you seem bored with the way the interview is moving, then you can politely say, "I'd like to change direction. May I ask another question?" Also, ask questions that require more than a one-word or yes/no explanation.

3. **Thank the person for sharing his or her time and expertise with you.** Ask your interviewee whether you can telephone or e-mail, when writing your narrative, if you need additional information.

4. **Send a final copy of the narrative to the interviewee.**

82   ©2000 Teacher Created Materials, Inc.

Standards and Benchmarks: 4A

Techniques for Nonfiction Narratives *(cont.)*

Writing Open-Ended Questions

Following is a list of interview questions that are poorly written. Why? They are poor because when asked these questions, the person can respond with a one-word or yes/no answer. It is far better to design open-ended questions that make the interviewee reveal and think about his or her responses. In return, you will have a detailed, thorough, and interesting interview. For these 10 questions, revise the wording of the questions so they are open-ended. Write new questions on the board and discuss variations. Also, discuss why these new questions would be good questions to ask in an interview.

1. Where did you grow up?

2. Did or do you go to school?

3. Are you pleased with your career choice?

4. Do you have a large family?

5. Do you have any hobbies?

6. Is your job challenging?

7. Did you have any pets when growing up? Do you have any now?

8. Do you consider yourself a good friend?

9. Where is your favorite place to go?

10. What is one goal you have?

Standards and Benchmarks: 1A, 1B, 1C, 1D, 1E, 1G, 1I, 1L, 2A, 2B, 2C, 2D, 3A, 3B, 3C, 3D, 3E, 3F, 3G, 3H, 3I, 3J, 3K, 3L, 4A, 4B, 4C, 4D, 4E, 4F, 4G, 4H

Role Model

Description

Write a nonfiction narrative about a role model.

Prewriting Activities

- As a class, define "Role Model" on the chalkboard and generate a list of positive role models. Next to each name, write the reasons why these people are positive influences.
- Make a personal list in your journals of positive role models you know. Choose one individual, and write why and how this person has affected you. Share with the class.
- Choose your number-one role model. Make three columns in your journal:

Things I Know   **Things I Want to Know**   **Things I Learned**

  List what you already know about the person in the first column, what you would like to know in the second column, and after finding the answers to what you wanted to know, list what you learned in the third column.

  Use this as a basis for gathering information about the role model selected.

- Create a character sketch for this person.
- Identify story: what makes this person a role model?

Three-Way Tie

Although he hesitates to get his briefcase and strides instead of runs to the front door, his jaw finally relaxes since leaving the city. He is home. Once his key unlocks the door, his role changes from businessman to father. Our father.

Three steps after the dog (which always hears the jingling keys first), we three boys run upstairs. We soar into his arms, clutch legs, and hang like chimpanzees from his tie—giving him an incentive to remove it and change into "Daddy" clothes, comfortable and comforting.

He becomes a bridge, and we crawl over and under, fighting for kisses, rejecting the kisses, but wanting more. He searches for bare bellies to blow bubbles, and collects tolls to let us "escape," then be pulled, by ankle or arm, into the monster's clutches for more kisses, more hugs, and more bubbles. Meetings, deadlines, and decisions vanish faster than the setting sun, and as the last of us is pried off, clinging tighter than a barnacle to the underside of a fishing trawler, we four "men" stumble into the kitchen, where food not only nourishes, but also provides time to talk about the day.

Dad always asks the questions, and we are eager to share our news and our world with him. Mom asks about his day, and he winks. That talk is saved for later. Those discussions are clandestine, and we boys never knew they existed.

Role Model *(cont.)*

Three-Way Tie *(cont.)*

Our family adventures included places where picnics could be brought, and distances where we drifted into dreamland in the car, yet always woke up in our own beds. School events were attended by both mom and dad, hand in hand, and Dad never once complained about missing work.

Somehow, he managed to coach our sports. A whistle, a navy sweat suit, and a baseball cap were his trademarks. Untied cleats were the only indication that his dressing wasn't done in the team locker room, but at the office. His cell phone beeped in the glove compartment, and at the end of practice or a game, one of us would see the blinking light and hand Dad the phone. Inevitably, Dad responded, "You boys are my business." And he'd return the phone to its spot.

The "roughhousing" of the past became arm wrestling matches and running races. Dad needed a partner on the basketball court instead of the three-on-one competitions.

Whether our teams won the trophies or whether or not we made the team, we three boys knew we were Dad's first-place prizes. He told us then, and he tells us now when he grabs the three of us in a bear hug, "My three-way tie." We squirm and resist, but hold him tighter as he whispers again, "My three-way-tie."

Discussion

- What is the theme of "Three-Way Tie"?
- Why is the father chosen as a positive role model?
- Free-write how your mother, father, or guardian is a positive role model. Share.

Writing

Write a nonfiction narrative about a role model. Your reasons why this person is a good influence should be supported with research.

Publishing

- Create a collage about your role model.
- Make a time line outlining this individual's life.

Technology Connections

- Word-process the narratives.
- Collect or take photographs of your role model. Scan the photographs to include in a multi-media presentation.

My Role Model Time Line

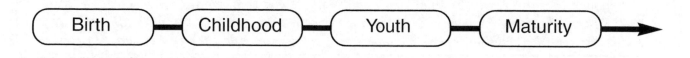

Birth — Childhood — Youth — Maturity →

 **Standards and Benchmarks:** 1A, 1B, 1C, 1D, 1E, 1G, 1I, 1L, 2A, 2B, 2C, 2D, 3A, 3B, 3C, 3D, 3E, 3F, 3G, 3H, 3I, 3J, 3K, 3L, 4A, 4B, 4C, 4D, 4E, 4F, 4G, 4H

Legends

Description

Write a nonfiction narrative about a legend in your family or from your culture or heritage which has been passed down through the generations.

Prewriting Activities

- Write "Legend" on the chalkboard and define it. A legend is a story handed down from the past, especially one that is widely believed but unverifiable.

- Students should share legends they know about their town, community, city, even school. Legends can be about people, places, and things.

Truth or Dare

Sam and Libby weren't supposed to be knee-deep in water at Crystal Lake, never mind how they had to get there—trespassing on Bartleby's property. But Libby dared him. And because Sam liked Libby so very, very much, how could he not fulfill her dare to swim at Crystal Lake? He knew how dangerous it was. His Great Aunt Martha had told him, unbeknownst to Sam's parents, and Sam had never forgotten.

Bartleby was the richest man this side, and probably the other side, too, of the Mississippi. He was a scientist who concocted a potion that kept a person alive forever. Only there was a glitch. The potion didn't stop aging! Unfortunately, Bartleby didn't realize this until after he had sipped his own potion.

Now the old-timers who gathered to play chess every Thursday morning in the gazebo that Bartleby's other inventions paid for, rarely mentioned his name. Maybe they knew one day they would die, and maybe they were jealous that Bartleby never would. Or maybe the thought of Bartleby decaying and rotting and not dying scared them so much they thought mentioning his name may give them the invisible sip of Bartleby's failed experiment. Whatever it was, just thinking about his appearance kept the land developers away from Bartleby's estate and kept Bartleby away from civilization.

Now, here they were, splashing each other in the cold water that made Libby arch her back and scream each time water landed on her. Sam knew he loved Libby. And Libby knew she loved Sam. The way he held her hand as he led her down the trails dotted with orange "Keep Out" signs. The way he observed the trees, half-expecting a decomposed Bartleby to pop out from behind one. Libby wished that Sam had asked her a "truth" question and that she had been brave enough to ask, "Do you like me?" instead of, "I dare you to swim at Crystal Lake." After all, Libby's grandparents had warned her parents who, in turn, warned Libby never ever to look in the direction of Bartleby's property because they said Bartleby was the Devil. Libby shivered.

86 ©2000 Teacher Created Materials, Inc.

Legends *(cont.)*

Truth or Dare *(cont.)*

"Truth is, Sam Pierce," Libby climbed on a rock and swore she heard the trees whisper her name, "I want to leave. You completed your dare."

The word "relief" practically spilled out of Sam. "Before we go, one last question. Or dare."

"I choose 'dare.' And hurry up!" Libby felt the wind grow stronger.

Sam wished Libby had said "truth" so he could have found out for sure whether she liked him, before he admitted that he liked her.

"Libby Curtis, I dare you to—" Just then, the wind slapped their faces, and a huge splash made from a boulder or monster or devil or someone with superhuman strength made them both scream and run, run, run through the brambles and over the twigs and past the "No Trespassing" signs until they were safe.

"My dad said Bartleby killed people," Libby breathed heavily.

"Mine, too." Sam leaned against a tree. "How about no more dares."

"Fine. Only truths." Libby shook her head as if shaking away the image of Bartleby.

"Truth is," Sam added, "I like you, Libby. And I'd do anything for you." Sam could hardly believe the words sputtering out of his mouth. It was as if the water at Crystal Lake had some magical power that made him tell Libby.

"Truth is," Libby had sipped some of the water, too, "I like you, Sam."

Sam and Libby both wondered if they would always tell the truth just like they were now, or if the truth serum Bartleby must have spilled into Crystal Lake would wear off. Only time would tell.

Discussion

- Discuss the legend of Bartleby and the power the legend has over the community.
- Discuss how Bartleby's legend will end, if ever.
- Discuss and list possible themes for "Truth or Dare."
- Make a list of truths you would like to ask certain people and a list of dares you would like to see other people complete. Discuss when it is time to "draw the line."
- Discuss with your family legends from your culture, background, religion, or ancestors. Choose one to answer *who, what, where, when, why,* and *how,* summarize, and then bring to class. Share.

Writing

Write about a legend, which you are presenting as nonfiction, from your culture, religion, or background. Include where the legend originated and how it has come to your knowledge.

Publishing

Write the legend as a children's book. Include illustrations. Include a dedication page. Share with lower grade levels. Share with the class.

Technology Connection

Experiment with fonts and clip art to make the children's book. Each page should include an illustration.

 **Standards and Benchmarks:** 1A, 1B, 1C, 1D, 1E, 1G, 1I, 1L, 2A, 2B, 2C, 2D, 3A, 3B, 3C, 3D, 3E, 3F, 3G, 3H, 3I, 3J, 3K, 3L, 4A, 4B, 4C, 4D, 4E, 4F, 4G, 4H

Historical Fiction

Description
Take one historical incident, research it, and "fictionalize" the narrative to make the reader feel a part of history.

Prewriting Activities
- Define historical fiction.
- List titles you have read or shows you have seen that are historical fiction.
- Discuss why authors might use the stylistic device of fictionalizing history.
- As class, brainstorm a list of historical events. Summarize historical events for each other. (The following list can serve as a source to draw from when trying to think of specific situations to consider for the narratives. The possibilities are obviously inexhaustible.)

Possible Topics and Persons to Consider

Revolutionary War	Gold Rush	Pocahontas
Civil War	Civil Rights Movement	Sacajawea
World War I	World Exploration	Lewis and Clark
World War II	Space Exploration	Crazy Horse
Korean War	Science Exploration	Sitting Bull
Vietnam War	Martin Luther King, Jr.	Geronimo
Gulf War	Harriet Tubman	Cochise
Olympic Games	Susan B. Anthony	Abraham Lincoln

- Brainstorm how the event could be fictionalized and discuss how fictionalizing could enhance the narrative.
- Students should choose one historical event and answer *who*, *what*, *where*, *when*, *why*, and *how*. Next, students should write a narrative summary. The summary should be researched for accuracy. Then share the narratives with the class. Create a plot jot for fictionalizing.

Writing
Compose a historical fiction narrative. Research must be conducted so that the event is depicted accurately. Weave fiction into the historical event, possibly through a real or imagined figure writing in a "diary." Bring the reader into the history. Also, you should provide a summary of the historical event in direct nonfiction.

Publishing
- Create a map, chart, or time line of your historical event.
- Present your narrative to the class dressed "in character" from your narrative.

Technology Connection
Write the nonfiction elements in italics and the fiction in regular print. Use a video camera to present your narrative. Write a script and enlist family and friends to play various roles. Show the dramatized story to the class.

 **Standards and Benchmarks:** 1A, 1B, 1C, 1D, 1E, 1G, 1I, 1L, 2A, 2B, 2C, 2D, 3A, 3B, 3C, 3D, 3E, 3F, 3G, 3H, 3I, 3J, 3K, 3L, 4A, 4B, 4C, 4D, 4E, 4F, 4G, 4H

Family Tree

Description

Write a nonfiction narrative about a living relative.

Prewriting Activities

- Complete the Family Tree Graphic Organizer (page 141). List the birthplace, occupation, and one interesting fact about each relative. Parental assistance may be necessary.
- Cluster the word "Family."
- Free-write to the question "What makes a family so important?" Share your response.
- Complete the Comparison Graphic Organizer (page 136) on similarities and differences between family and friends. From the graphic organizer, write a comparison/contrast paragraph to share.
- Choose one living relative whom you find interesting. After completing a character sketch on this relative, begin to identify a story about the relative. Prepare a list of interview questions to gather information before composing the narrative. Conduct the interview.

Writing

Write a narrative about an interesting relative. The topic of the narrative may vary greatly. You may write about a funny, sad, painful, memorable experience, or about this relative's childhood, hobby, occupation, or simply a story—the awkward moment at a restaurant the night before, perhaps. The point is that students need to find a topic interesting to them, so that others are interested too.

Publishing

Make a creative "family tree" to submit with the narrative. Share the nonfiction narrative with that relative. Share this relative's comments with the class.

Technology Connections

- Word-process the narrative.
- Use the Internet to assist in locating names and information. Use "Family Tree" software programs.
- Collect photographs of family members, scan, and create a multi-media presentation on your family. Present this to your family and, perhaps, to the class.

 **Standards and Benchmarks:** 1A, 1B, 1C, 1D, 1E, 1G, 1I, 2A, 2B, 2C, 2D, 3A, 3B, 3C, 3D, 3E, 3F, 3G, 3H, 3I, 3J, 3K, 3L, 4A, 4B, 4C, 4D, 4E, 4F, 4G, 4H

Environmental Awareness

Description

Write a nonfiction narrative about an environmental issue.

Prewriting Activities

- As a class, brainstorm environmental issues. List these on the chalkboard. Copy these in your notebooks. Consider the following possible issues: animals and vegetation which are extinct or on the verge of extinction, clear-cutting/deforestation, illegal dumping, toxic waste, emissions/vehicle standards, preservation of the rain forest, pollution, acid rain, recycling centers, etc.

- Define and give examples of the issues.

- Write "Our Environment" in your journal. Cluster this term. Based on offshoots, identify topics. Choose one topic from the cluster and write a paragraph. Share with the class.

- Choose one environmental issue that is important to you and make a list of reasons telling why the issue is important.

Writing

Write a narrative about an environmental issue. The first step is defining the issue. Step two is writing all the reasons why this issue is important. Step three is gathering information and documenting sources. Step four is identifying a story—perhaps locating someone who is dedicated to this environmental issue or writing the "history" of the environmental issue. For instance, how did we discover the effects of acid rain? And how are we trying to remedy the situation? Are the remedies working? What will happen in the future?

Publishing

Create a poster about your environmental issue to raise awareness. Include at least three facts/pieces from your narrative. Display the posters in your classroom or school. Share the narratives with the class. Use the poster as a visual aid.

Technology Connections

- Word-process the narrative.
- Create a Web site on your environmental issue. Include your narrative.

 **Standards and Benchmarks:** 1A, 1B, 1C, 1D, 1E, 1G, 1I, 2A, 2B, 2C, 2D 3A, 3B, 3C, 3D, 3E, 3F, 3G, 3H, 3I, 3J, 3K, 3L, 4A, 4B, 4C, 4D, 4E, 4F, 4G, 4H

Greatest Invention

Description

Write a nonfiction narrative about what you consider to be the greatest invention and include personal anecdotes sharing their reasons why the invention is great.

Prewriting Activities

- Complete the Comparison Graphic Organizer (page 136) comparing nonfiction and fiction.

- Discuss how the inclusion of personal opinions in nonfiction enhances or detracts from narratives.

- Brainstorm a class list of greatest inventions in two categories—greatest inventions for you personally and greatest inventions for the world in general. Students should give reasons why these inventions are great. Analyze how the inventions differ for the two categories.

- Choose one favorite invention, either for the world or for you, and in one paragraph tell why this invention is terrific.

- Research the invention, the inventor, why the invention was developed in the first place, and how it has benefited either you or society, using various sources for information.

  Take, for example, Henry Ford of the Ford Motor Company, whose business success was partly due to his belief that "A man can never leave his business. He ought to think of it by day and dream of it by night."

- Use the Greatest Invention Preparation Outline (page 92) to organize your notes.

Writing

Compose a nonfiction narrative telling the circumstances leading up to a particular invention and how the invention has proven beneficial. Within the nonfiction narrative, add personal comments as to how you have benefited from the invention. Decide whether the inclusion of personal comments enhances a narrative.

Publishing

- Create an advertisement for this invention. Include several facts from the narrative.

- Create a time line for the invention process. Draw a picture of the greatest invention.

Technology Connections

- Produce commercials for the greatest invention, using video cameras.

- Record "radio spots" for your greatest inventions. Try for one 30-second spot and one 60-second spot.

Greatest Invention *(cont.)*

Preparation Outline

The greatest invention is . . .

_____

I think this is the greatest invention because of the following reasons:

    1. _____

    2. _____

    3. _____

Others think this is a great invention because of the following reasons:

    1. _____

    2. _____

    3. _____

The inventor is (was) _____

The inventor invented this because of the following reasons:

_____

_____

Interesting facts about the inventor's life:

_____

_____

Steps leading up to the invention:

_____

_____

Other achievements of the inventor:

_____

_____

_____

_____

 **Standards and Benchmarks:** 1A, 1B, 1C, 1D, 1E, 1G, 1I, 2A, 2B, 2C, 2D 3A, 3B, 3C, 3D, 3E, 3F, 3G, 3H, 3I, 3J, 3K, 3L, 4A, 4B, 4C, 4D, 4E, 4F, 4G, 4H

Support the Arts

Description

Write a biographical narrative about one individual involved in the arts—painter, sculptor, musician, author, architect, interior or fashion designer, chef, dancer, actor, or graphic artist.

Prewriting Activities

- Divide a journal into 10 sections. Label each section with one of the individuals listed above.

- Under each category, name people you know or have heard of who have made contributions to society with their talents.

Sampling of Names from the Arts

Rembrandt	Gucci	Weber	Copland
Hawthorne	Whistler	Schubert	Wolfgang Puck
Bach	Steinbeck	Donna Karan	Paul Prudhomme
Frank Lloyd Wright	Mozart	Calvin Klein	E. A. Poe
Picasso	Dior	Andrew Wyeth	Chopin
Shakespeare	Gainsborough	Paul McCartney	Agnes De Mille
Beethoven	Mark Twain	Dickens	Twyla Tharpe
I. M. Pei	Stravinsky	Winslow Homer	Brahms
Van Gogh	Tommy Hilfiger	Verdi	Emerson
Hemingway	Grant Wood	Gershwin	Elgar

Choose one individual from any of the representative categories to write a nonfiction narrative about. Gather information, identify the story, and draft the narrative. Complete a character sketch to bring the particular artist to life. Make sure your conflict is presented early (so the reader is intrigued) and then show the steps leading to the conflict's resolution.

Publishing

- Create a time line listing the individual's significant moments.

Technology Connections

- Word-process the narratives.

- Using PowerPoint® (or a similar application), create a minimum of five slides on the individual. Present these to the class. Give this collection to the library for other students to use as references.

Standards and Benchmarks: 1A, 1B, 1C, 1D, 1E, 1G, 1I, 1L, 2A, 2B, 2C, 2D, 3A, 3B, 3C, 3D, 3E, 3F, 3G, 3H, 3I, 3J, 3K, 3L, 4A, 4B, 4C, 4D, 4E, 4F, 4G

Things I Never Knew About My Family

Description:

Write about a deceased family member and compose a biographical narrative.

Prewriting Activities

- List relatives who have died. Next to each name, write anything you can remember about this individual. Perhaps another relative has told about him or her.
- Using the Family Tree Graphic Organizer (page 141), students should choose one deceased family member whom they wish to remember through a biography.

The Jungle Bath

Uncle Sal wears "happy glasses," and I love to be around him. He makes everything funny, and whatever problem I may have, after I tell Uncle Sal about it, somehow he makes it vanish.

One day my mom came home in an awful mood. Someone else got the promotion she felt belonged to her.

"Hey, Ma," I said, "when the hippo runs out of soap, he'll ask the ostrich to share some of his."

My mother looked at me, and said, "What?"

"Uncle Sal always tells me that when I'm down, and it makes me laugh. You've never heard the hippo story? Well, the ostrich never gives him the soap, and the hippo—" I giggled, picturing Uncle Sal as a hippo, enlarging his mouth so every molar and cavity are exposed, and then craning his neck and strutting like an ostrich, pecking, "Soap, share some soap? Just who does that hippo think he is?"

"What does the story mean, exactly?" my mother asked, a dozen lines on her forehead, to which Uncle Sal would remark, "Plantin' time already, big sis? Whaddaya harvestin' this season?"

"Um, I don't actually know," I offered, but continued in the best Uncle Sal imitation I could muster, "And if ya put on them happy glasses, you won't be sad anymore!"

"Your Uncle Sal is crazy." Mom stormed out of the kitchen.

"He is crazy, and that's why I like him! 'Cause nothing bothers him or worries him and he makes me laugh!" I yelled. Sure, I felt bad that my ma didn't get the promotion, but, to quote another Uncle Sal-ism, "If you worry too much about today, and can't forget yesterday, then tomorrow brings more bad weather."

Growing up, my best memories included Uncle Sal. He pretended to be Santa Claus almost the whole month of December. In February, he turned into Cupid, shooting fake darts at people he thought should be in love.

"Uncle Sal, why don't you let me shoot an arrow at you?" I aimed my finger at him.

©2000 Teacher Created Materials, Inc.

Things I Never Knew About My Family *(cont.)*

The Jungle Bath *(cont.)*

A dark cloud passed over Uncle Sal. It was a stern, gloomy look. For the first time, I recognized the similarity between him and my mother. Ma looked like that half the time. She worried constantly.

"Hey, Uncle Sal!" I feigned punches and dodged his invisible uppercuts.

It was as if I had pushed the "on" button. Sal continued shooting arrows at the passers-by, and whispered in my ear as I hugged him goodbye later that day, "I got you, kid. Whaddaya think I need love for?"

Uncle Sal became Abe Lincoln, Martin Luther King, Jr., and Christopher Columbus on their respective holidays. He made us celebrate Cinco de Mayo, which became a new family tradition, and at all family birthdays, Uncle Sal had to be first at the games, shattering the piñata or pinning the tail on the donkey. Even now that we're too old for party games, it is Sal who initiates and insists that we all participate. We always do. Uncle Sal makes it fun.

On Halloween, Uncle Sal actually collects candy! He is so cool, my friends beg me weeks in advance to accompany us trick-or-treating. His costumes are awesome, and he plans next year's costume sometime in the summer!

My ma returned to the kitchen and knelt beside me. "Kiddo," Ma rubbed my back, "You know, Uncle Sal really is crazy."

"I know." I smiled. "I want to be just like him when I grow up. Nothing bothers him, Ma. I love you, you know that, but Uncle Sal is always happy!"

Ma rested her head on my back and whispered, "Kiddo, your Uncle Sal, my baby brother, is crazy."

The way she said "crazy" bothered me. "Crazy" suddenly took on more meaning than just silliness, or enthusiasm. "Crazy" now meant insane.

"He's not," I choked. "Crazy people live in weird places and wear straitjackets and eat beetles and don't make any sense—"

"No, they don't. Uncle Sal has bipolar disorder, borderline schizophrenia. Medication helps." My ma paused, and I could see the pain and sadness in her eyes. I could also see my reflection in her eyes, and tears fell from both of us.

"He's not crazy," I blurted.

"You're right," my mother agreed. "He has a mental illness. And it doesn't mean we don't love him anymore with our whole hearts. I just wanted you to understand that when Uncle Sal wears his happy glasses, invisible to you and me, he truly believes he is wearing glasses. Uncle Sal's world is real to him. He believes he is the Easter Bunny, or George Washington, or Uncle Sam. That is what makes our Sal so special. That is why you love him so much. Because he lets you escape with him. But kiddo, his world is primarily fantasy."

"So, are you telling me he doesn't know who I am?" I could barely talk.

Things I Never Knew About My Family *(cont.)*

The Jungle Bath *(cont.)*

"No!" my ma corrected, "He loves you and invites you into his world because of his love for you! You are his incentive to continue medication and seek counseling! He knows you, don't ever doubt that."

"I love him, Ma." I held onto her and cried.

"And you always should," Ma said.

"I love that he's crazy. He wouldn't be Uncle Sal if he wasn't. He'd be the same as all of us. Uncle Sal loves everyone, and everyone loves him. If that's bipolar or schizo-whatever-you-call-it, then I want to be just like him—I do!"

"I know," Mom said. "His world is often better than ours. But we're in the real world and must deal with our obstacles and problems. Sometimes I wish I did have a pair of happy glasses, but I don't. It's not that simple."

Neither of us spoke. I can't say what my ma thought, but I could only think of that hippo in his jungle pool running out of soap and asking the ostrich to share. The ostrich doesn't, and I finally understood why. The hippo spends his whole life in the jungle pool, bathing with soap. When he runs out, he believes he can't function without the bar of soap, so he asks the ostrich, who rarely bathes. When the ostrich does not share, the hippo's routine is altered. He could sit in his pool all day and worry about not getting a bar of soap, or he could enjoy the day and make the most of it. Without the soap, the hippo will still be a hippo.

Uncle Sal is smarter than most of us "normal" people.

My mother turned to me. "Whaddaya say we chuck those leftovers and take your Uncle Sal a pepperoni pizza?"

I wipe my eyes with the back of my hands and nod in agreement.

"Maybe we'll stop at the store and get us a six-pack of soap!" My ma laughs, and her worry lines disappear.

Uncle Sal always makes us smile. And there's nothing wrong with that.

Discussion

- Why does the narrator first accept and later reject the word "crazy" for Uncle Sal?
- What is the theme of "Jungle Bath"?

Writing

Write a biographical narrative on a deceased relative, showing why this person is important to remember and telling an intriguing story everyone can learn from.

Publishing

Word-process the narrative and send it to relatives.

Technology Connection

E-mail the narrative to family members.

 ©2000 Teacher Created Materials, Inc.

Standards and Benchmarks: 1A, 1B, 1C, 1D, 1E, 1I, 2A, 2B, 2C, 2D, 3A, 3B, 3C, 3D, 3E, 3F, 3G, 3H, 3I, 3J, 3K, 3L, 4A, 4B, 4C, 4D, 4E, 4F, 4G, 4H

My Friend and My Future

Description #1 (My Friend)

Interview a friend and create a biographical narrative about this friend.

Prewriting Activities

- Free-write about an experience you have had with a friend whom you will always remember.
- Choose one friend whom you would like to interview. Complete a character sketch of this friend. List three or more memories you have with this friend.
- Before designing interview questions, answer the following, "Why am I interviewing this friend?" Formulate the questions. Conduct the interview.

Writing

Using interview responses, identify a story about your friend that is worthy of a narrative.

Publishing

Share the narratives with the class.

Technology Connection

- Word-process the narrative.
- Collect pictures of your special friend. Scan. Use one picture (or a selected group of pictures) as the center of a poster. Write several adjectives about this friend around the photograph. Use as a cover for the narrative.

Description #2 (My Future)

Students will write a nonfiction narrative about a person whose occupation they are considering for future employment.

Prewriting Activities

- As class, brainstorm a list of occupations on the chalkboard. Define them.
- Choose one occupation you may consider when you "grow up" and free-write the reason why you may choose to pursue this line of work.
- Locate a person in the area with this occupation, and then interview the person if possible. Or, find a prominent person in this line of work from whom to conduct research.

Writing

Write a nonfiction narrative about one person who has an appealing occupation.

Publishing

Invite individuals upon whom the narratives are based to come in for "Career Day." Your narrative will be read as introduction. The class can then ask questions about that career.

Technology Connections

- Word-process the narratives.
- Create a multimedia presentation about the career in your narrative. Using at least six slides, identify the steps or processes involved in obtaining this type of occupation.

Standards and Benchmarks: 1B, 1C, 1D, 2A, 2B, 2C, 2D, 3A, 3B, 3C, 3D, 3E, 3F, 3G, 3H, 3I, 3J, 3K, 3L, 4A, 4B, 4C, 4D, 4E, 4F, 4G, 4H

Reader Response Check Sheet

1. What did you learn from the narrative? _____

2. Was the plot in sequential order? _____ Was it logical? _____
   Did the narrative flow? _____
   Beginning:_____
   Middle: _____
   Climax: _____
   End: _____

3. Describe how the characters were portrayed so they seemed real: _____
   _____

4. Was the setting well described?_____

5. What was your first impression of the title? _____

6. How did the first paragraph pique your interest? _____

7. Figurative Language Examples:_____
   _____
   _____

8. Sensory Imagery Examples: _____
   _____
   _____

9. Action Verbs: _____
   _____
   _____

10. Was the conflict introduced at the beginning of the narrative? What was the conflict, type of conflict, and how was the conflict resolved? _____
    _____

11. Were facts properly documented within the narrative? Did the inclusion of references maintain the pace of the narrative? _____

12. Is the bibliography in proper format and representative of a variety of sources? _____
    _____

13. Spelling/Punctuation: _____

14. What would you do to revise the narrative? _____

15. List three strengths of the narrative:_____
    _____
    _____

Assessment Rubric

The rubric is weighted at 100%. Ten is the highest single rating. Add up numbers to get a total score.

1. All prewriting activities were completed. 10 9 8 7 6 5 4 3 2 1 0			
2. Research was gathered from a variety of sources. 10 9 8 7 6 5 4 3 2 1 0			
3. The bibliography is listed and written in proper format. 10 9 8 7 6 5 4 3 2 1 0			
4. The narrative tells a story, complete with conflict, characters, setting, and theme. 10 9 8 7 6 5 4 3 2 1 0			
5. The narrative has a beginning, middle, climax, and end that follow sequentially. 10 9 8 7 6 5 4 3 2 1 0			
6. Research is correctly documented within the narrative. 10 9 8 7 6 5 4 3 2 1 0			
7. Figurative language, sensory imagery, and strong action verbs contribute to the narrative. 10 9 8 7 6 5 4 3 2 1 0			
8. Spelling and punctuation are accurate. 10 9 8 7 6 5 4 3 2 1 0			
9. The revision process shows attention and insight. 10 9 8 7 6 5 4 3 2 1 0			
10. Overall presentation is word-processed and follows guidelines. 10 9 8 7 6 5 4 3 2 1 0			
(If no interview was conducted, add five points to #8 and #9.) Total Score			

The Fairy Tale

Fairy tales are fictional narratives based on an enchanting land—Fairyland! Most fairy tales are set long, long ago, once upon a time, in a land far away. Fairy tales have real and imaginative characters who can interact and communicate with each other. Most fairy tales have children or young adults as their heroines and heroes, and parents, stepparents, or guardians are minor figures in the story. The main character must battle conflicts alone or with the help of elves, sprites, fairies, pixies, and the like. Fairy tales are often "rags to riches" stories—where the character begins poor and rises to royalty by means of the "happily-ever-after" ending. Good always defeats evil in fairy tales.

Scholars tell us that fairy tales have a long history, coming down to us from the mists of the past, most of the European classics stemming from the fertile imaginations of ancient cultures. The best known collectors of such tales, of course, were the famed Brothers Grimm—Jakob and Wilhelm—philologists and folklorists who did most of their work in the first half of the nineteenth century.

- To introduce Fairy Tale Narrative Writing, the class should generate a list of familiar fairy tales. A beginning sample list appears below.
- Summarize the fairy tales using the 5W+H method (who, what, where, when, why, and how).
- Meet in groups and divide the listed fairy tales among the groups. The groups should read their fairy tales and complete the Fairy Tale Prewriting Fact Sheet on page 101.

Sample List of Best Known Fairy Tales
Goldilocks and the Three Bears
Little Red Riding Hood
Hansel and Gretel
Jack and the Beanstalk
Rumpelstiltskin
The Three Billy Goats Gruff
The Little Gingerbread Man
Snow White
Puss in Boots
Beauty and the Beast
The Three Little Pigs
Cinderella
Tom Thumb
The Pied Piper
The Princess and the Pea
The Elves and the Shoemaker
The Frog Prince
The Emperor's New Clothes
The Golden Goose
Rapunzel

 ©2000 Teacher Created Materials, Inc.

Standards and Benchmarks: 1A, 1L

Fairy Tale Prewriting Fact Sheet

❑ **Name of the fairy tale:** _____

❑ **Characters:** List five traits for each character.

	Character 1	Character 2	Character 3	Character 4
Name				
Trait 1:				
Trait 2:				
Trait 3:				
Trait 4:				
Trait 5:				

❑ Setting:

❑ Conflict(s):

❑ Plot:

❑ Theme:

❑ Evidence of theme:

 **Standards and Benchmarks:** 1A, 1B, 1C, 1D, 1E, 1G, 1L, 2A, 2B, 2C, 2D 3A, 3B, 3C, 3D, 3E, 3F, 3G, 3H, 3I, 3J, 3K, 3L

Personal Fairy Tale

Description (Version #1)

Write a personal fairy tale based upon a classic fairy tale.

Prewriting Activities

- Choose one fairy tale that has a plot resembling an incident from your personal life. The plot doesn't have to be exact, but instances must be similar. For example, in "Hansel and Gretel," the main characters get left in the woods to fend for themselves. Perhaps this reminds you of a time you were at the mall and "lost" your parents, and someone offered you a ride home—which, of course, you politely declined. After all, it may have been the evil witch! You can surely empathize with the feelings of Hansel and Gretel!
- Identify *who, what, where, when, why,* and *how* of your personal experience.

Writing

Write your personal fairy tale narrative.

Publishing

Share the fairy tales. See if the class can identify which fairy tale yours resembles.

Technology Connection

- Word-process. Use a "fairy tale font"—something ornate or fancy. Find clip art to include.
- Create a cover using a graphics program.

Description (Version #2)

Compose a personal fairy tale based on an original plot.

Prewriting Activities

- As a class, think of possible titles for original fairy tales. List them on the chalkboard. Some examples might be "The Dangerous Dungeon," "The Moat Monster," "The Princess in the Tower," "The Evil in the Wood," "The Sorcerer's Magic," "The Deserted Castle," etc.
- Choose one title and write a plot jot for it. Share with the class.
- Complete a Fairy Tale Prewriting Fact Sheet for the original idea.

Writing

Compose an original fairy tale.

Publishing

Illustrate your fairy tale and read it to lower grade levels.

Technology Connections

- Word-process with a unique font.
- Use clip art to include in your fairy tale. Use borders, enlarge the first letter of each paragraph, and create a cover, using a graphics program.

Standards and Benchmarks: 1A, 1B, 1C, 1D, 1E, 1G, 1L, 2A, 2B, 2C, 2D, 3A, 3B, 3C, 3D, 3E, 3F, 3G, 3H, 3I, 3J, 3K, 3L

New Perspective Fairy Tale

Description (Version #1)

Write a fairy tale from a different point of view.

Prewriting Activities

- List three favorite fairy tales in three columns in your journals. Next, choose one character from each fairy tale who will be writing the same story, but from a different viewpoint. Write in the columns how each story will change with a different narrator.
- Identify story parts—beginning, middle, climax, and end—and write possible variations.
- Choose one classic fairy tale and one new character from the tale to rewrite the story. Complete the Fairy Tale Prewriting Fact Sheet (page 101) as a guide before writing.

Writing

Rewrite a fairy tale from another character's point of view. Remember, the plot must stay the same; however, it is viewed through another's eyes. Before beginning, complete a character sketch of that character. All information should be filled in because you are that character!

Publishing

Dress up as the character and tell your side of the story.

Technology Connection

- Word-process the narratives.
- Students should illustrate the fairy tale, using a graphics program.

Description (Version #2)

Students will rewrite a classic fairy tale to end *unhappily* ever after.

Prewriting Activities

- Complete the Fairy Tale Prewriting Fact Sheet on one fairy tale you would like to see end "unhappily ever after."
- Free-write why the particular fairy tale should not end happily.

Writing

Rewrite one classic fairy tale to end unhappily. How does the climax change? How do the characters react to the new climax? If using the traditional climax, will the fairy tale make sense with an unhappy ending?

Publishing

Students should illustrate and read the new endings to fairy tales.

Technology Connection

- Word-process the fairy tales.
- Students should use *KidPix*® (or similar application) to create the new "unhappy" ending for others to read.

Standards and Benchmarks: 1A, 1B, 1C, 1D, 1E, 1G, 1L, 2A, 2B, 2C, 2D, 3A, 3B, 3C, 3D, 3E, 3F, 3G, 3H, 3I, 3J, 3K, 3L

Rhyming Fairy Tale

Description

Rewrite a fairy tale in rhyme.

Prewriting Activities

- Choose a fairy tale they wish to rewrite in rhyming verse.
- First paraphrase the fairy tale. Otherwise, the rhyming may become too difficult, due to the length of the tale.
- A sample starter verse appears below:

Little Red Riding Hood

A little girl, all dressed in red,
Visited Granny, sick in bed.
With a basket, filled with treats,
She walked the path, only to meet—
A Big Bad Wolf with a hungry stare,
But he told a joke so she didn't care.
Red thought, "He's funny, I should be nice!"
And gave him some juice without any ice.
"Thank you," said the wolf, "you are so kind."
"You're welcome," said Red, "now to Granny's to dine!"
The wolf found a shortcut and rushed ahead.
Whom would he eat first—Granny or Little Red?

- Finish the *Little Red Riding Hood* rhyme. Share your endings with the class.

Writing

Rewrite a classic fairy tale in rhyming verse. Have fun with the classic tale, altering it in any acceptable way you wish.

Publishing

- Read the rhymes to the class.
- Illustrate rhymes.

Technology Connection

Word-process the fairy tale rhymes. Experiment with font, justification, and page set-up.

Standards and Benchmarks: 1A, 1B, 1C, 1D, 1E, 1G, 1L   2A, 2B, 2C, 2D
3A, 3B, 3C, 3D, 3E, 3F, 3G, 3H, 3I, 3J, 3K, 3L

Jumbled Fairy Tale

Description
Jumble a classic fairy tale to create an unusual, original narrative.

Prewriting Activities
- Distribute Fairy Tale Prewriting Fact Sheets (page 101).
- On slips of paper or cards, the teacher will provide individual classic fairy tale titles. (There should be more titles than the number of students in the room.) The card you choose will determine the theme for your jumbled up fairy tale. Choose one card and copy the title. This card will be the basis for the plot. Fill in the plot on the Prewriting Fact Sheet. If you are unclear as to the plot of the assigned tale, research and read the story. Return the card to the stack.
- The card you choose next will determine the conflict for your jumbled up narrative. Identify the conflict(s) for the tale assigned. Return the card to the stack.
- The card you choose next determines the setting for your jumbled up fairy tale. Write down the setting. Return the card to the stack.
- Next, choose from the fairy tale character names on slips of paper. Choose four slips of paper. These are the four characters in your jumbled up fairy tale. Return the papers for the next student after using the characters on the Prewriting Fact Sheet.

Teacher Note: Sets of cards for fairy tales, themes, characters, conflicts, and settings are provided on pages 106–111. Use a different color for each set of cards. The theme cards are provided as a help and are keyed to the particular fairy tale by number. Additional cards may be prepared by using copies of the blank cards provided on each of the same pages. Duplicate these pages.

Writing
Using the Fairy Tale Prewriting Fact Sheet on page 101, compose a jumbled up fairy tale. You must weave all information in to create a logical, albeit odd, fairy tale. Think about which characters are good and which are evil. Think about how your setting can assimilate into the plot. Be sure you alter the plot as necessary to reflect theme.

Publishing
Read your jumbled-up fairy tale to the class.

Technology Connections
- Word-process your fairy tale.
- Create original theme music with lyrics to add to your fairy tale.

Title Card
Goldilocks and the Three Bears

Setting Card
Palace on a Stormy Night

Theme Card
The fox is a wily creature. Don't trust just anyone who pretends to be your friend.

Conflict Card
Person vs. Machine

Jumbled Fairy Tale *(cont.)*

Fairy Tale Title Cards

1. **Goldilocks and the Three Bears**	2. **Little Red Riding Hood**	3. **Hansel and Gretel**
4. **Jack and the Beanstalk**	5. **Rumpelstiltskin**	6. **The Three Billy Goats Gruff**
7. **The Little Gingerbread Man**	8. **Snow White**	9. **Puss in Boots**
10. **Beauty and the Beast**	11. **The Three Little Pigs**	12. **Cinderella**
13. **Tom Thumb**	14. **The Pied Piper**	15. **The Princess and the Pea**
16. **The Elves and the Shoemaker**	17. **The Frog Prince**	18. **The Emperor's New Clothes**
19. **The Golden Goose**	20. **Rapunzel**	**Title Cards**

©2000 Teacher Created Materials, Inc.

Jumbled Fairy Tale *(cont.)*

Fairy Tale Setting Cards		
1. **a cottage in the woods**	2. **woods and a cottage in the village**	3. **a gingerbread house in the forest**
4. **a house and a garden**	5. **a room filled with straw in a little house in a valley**	6. **a hillside and a bridge over a stream**
7. **a little old house in the countryside and a stream nearby**	8. **a forest, a wee house, and a castle**	9. **fields, a countryside, and a giant's castle**
10. **a dark forest and enchanted palace with gardens**	11. **three houses—one of straw, one of sticks, and one of brick**	12. **a house, a kitchen, and a palace**
13. **a peasant home, a farm, and a forest**	14. **a river, a hillside, and the town of Hamelin**	15. **a palace on a stormy night**
16. **a cottage with a shoemaker's shop**	17. **a palace in a shady forest with a cool pond**	18. **a palace and the streets of the city**
19. **a forest and inn, a city and palace**	20. **a great tower in the forest**	**Setting Cards**

Jumbled Fairy Tale *(cont.)*

Fairy Tale Theme Cards

1. **Never go off into the woods alone.**	2. **Don't talk to strangers.**	3. **There is evil in the world. Be observant and help one another.**
4. **It is possible for a lazy and disobedient son to learn to become kind and loving to his mother.**	5. **Unfair bargains—especially those using children as pawns—are evil.**	6. **Being too greedy and cruel will bring punishment.**
7. **The fox is a wily creature. Don't trust just anyone who pretends to be your friend.**	8. **Jealousy can be an evil thing.**	9. **Appearance can change one's fortune greatly.**
10. **Happiness is built on goodness, and true love depends on inner beauty—not outer good looks.**	11. **Be prudent and think ahead for safety and security.**	12. **A loving and dutiful daughter can charm a husband and even nasty sisters. Goodness will be rewarded.**
13. **Love of family is our highest value. Many dangers and evils exist in the outside world.**	14. **Don't cheat others, or you may lose your own dearest possessions.**	15. **"Real" royalty is not detected by outside appearance; it is determined by tender and sensitive feelings.**
16. **Honesty, hard work, generosity, and gratitude will pay off.**	17. **Keep your promises and be faithful, and you will be rewarded.**	18. **Vanity and the desire to go along with other's opinions (especially when they seem obviously wrong) can make a complete fool of a person.**
19. **A good-hearted fool can be a better person (and may even succeed to higher levels) than an ungenerous clever one.**	20. **True love will overcome ill fortune, blindness, jealousy, etc.**	**Theme Cards**

©2000 Teacher Created Materials, Inc.

Jumbled Fairy Tale *(cont.)*

Fairy Tale Character Cards		
1. **a little girl with golden hair**	2. **a mama bear, papa bear, and baby bear**	3. **a piper dressed in a scarlet and gold cloak**
4. **a gingerbread man**	5. **a widow**	6. **a lazy, disobedient boy**
7. **a cruel giant**	8. **a sly fox**	9. **three billy goats**
10. **a cat dressed in boots**	11. **a troll**	12. **three beautiful daughters**
13. **an ugly beast with a dreadful voice**	14. **a tiny little boy—very tiny but perfect**	15. **a poor peasant and his wife**
16. **two robbers**	17. **a milkmaid**	18. **a squire with a cow**
19. **two clever sons and a fool**	20. **a wicked wolf**	21. **a poor miller**

Jumbled Fairy Tale *(cont.)*

Fairy Tale Character Cards *(cont.)*

22. **a sick grandmother**	23. **two woodcutters**	24. **a king**
25. **a good queen**	26. **a wicked queen**	27. **seven dwarfs**
28. **three little pigs**	29. **a slimy frog**	30. **a young prince**
31. **an enchantress (Dame Gothe)**	32. **a girl with long, long golden hair (Rapunzel)**	33. **a poor little brother and sister (Hansel and Gretel)**
34. **a wicked witch**	35. **a rain-soaked, bedraggled-looking princess**	36. **a vain emperor**
37. **two rascal tailors**	38. **a poor little stepsister (Cinderella)**	39. **a fairy godmother**
40. **an old shoemaker**	41. **two elves in ragged clothes**	**Character Cards**

©2000 Teacher Created Materials, Inc.

Jumbled Fairy Tale *(cont.)*

Fairy Tale Conflict Cards *(cont.)*

Person vs. Person	Person vs. Machine	Person vs. Nature
Person vs. Self	Person vs. Society	Person vs. Person
Person vs. Machine	Person vs. Nature	Person vs. Self
Person vs. Society	Person vs. Person	Person vs. Machine
Person vs. Nature	Person vs. Self	Person vs. Society
Person vs. Person	Person vs. Machine	Person vs. Nature
Person vs. Self	Person vs. Society	Conflict Cards

Standards and Benchmarks: 1A, 1B, 1C, 1D, 1E, 1L, 2A, 2B, 2C, 2D, 3A, 3B, 3C, 3D, 3E, 3F, 3G, 3H, 3I, 3J, 3K, 3L

Reader Response Check Sheet

1. What was the theme of the fairy tale? Give an example from the fairy tale to support the theme._____

   _____

2. Was the plot in sequential order? _____

   Identify the parts of the story:

   Beginning:_____

   Middle: _____

   Climax: _____

   End: _____

3. Describe two of the characters: _____

4. Describe the setting: _____

5. Was the conflict introduced at the beginning of the fairy tale? What was the conflict, the type of conflict, and the conflict's resolution?_____

6. Was the dialogue realistic? Did dialogue enhance the fairy tale? If there is no dialogue, would the inclusion of dialogue be beneficial?_____

7. How did the title relate to the fairy tale? Was the title intriguing?_____

8. How did the first paragraph catch your attention and encourage you to read? _____

9. Figurative Language Examples:_____

   Sensory Imagery Examples: _____

   Action Verbs: _____

10. Spelling/Punctuation: _____

11. What would you do to revise the fairy tale? _____

12. List three strengths of the fairy tale:_____

   _____

   _____

112   ©2000 Teacher Created Materials, Inc.

Assessment Rubric

The rubric is weighted at 100%. Ten is the highest single score. Add up the numbers to get a total score.

1. All prewriting activities were completed.											
10	9	8	7	6	5	4	3	2	1	0	
2. During the revision process, the fairy tale shows not only revision but also incorporation of reader response comments.											
10	9	8	7	6	5	4	3	2	1	0	
3. The theme is clear without being stated.											
10	9	8	7	6	5	4	3	2	1	0	
4. The first paragraph/part of the narrative is intriguing and draws the reader in, and the conflict is presented.											
10	9	8	7	6	5	4	3	2	1	0	
5. The characters are lively, realistic, and their descriptions are true to their action.											
10	9	8	7	6	5	4	3	2	1	0	
6. The setting is clear and described so we can visualize it.											
10	9	8	7	6	5	4	3	2	1	0	
7. All parts of a story (beginning, middle, climax, and end) follow sequentially. The conflict is resolved.											
10	9	8	7	6	5	4	3	2	1	0	
8. Figurative language, sensory imagery, and strong action verbs contribute to the story.											
10	9	8	7	6	5	4	3	2	1	0	
9. Spelling and punctuation are correct.											
10	9	8	7	6	5	4	3	2	1	0	
10. The overall presentation of the narrative is word-processed and published according to directions.											
10	9	8	7	6	5	4	3	2	1	0	
										Total Score	

Standards and Benchmarks: 1A

Prewriting Activities

A conventional way of teaching literature has been to ask students to write expository analyses of stories, novels, and poems. In the narrative writing approach, however, the student is placed directly into the action, scene, thoughts, and dialogue of the story. This becomes a literary form of role playing—at once dramatic and analytical. Moreover, by becoming submerged in the story events, the student is using analytical tools almost without realizing it. And the end result, of course, is that the student is learning first-rate narrative writing skills while at the same time enjoying the appreciation of good literature. The ideal merger of creative and analytical writing takes place in this type of narrative writing about literature.

Some specific activities that promote this ideal merger are to ask students to write brief narratives which serve to compare specific characters, to show specific characters' reactions to a climax, to change a climax by introducing another character (oneself, perhaps), to rewrite a scene, to create an interior monologue for a character, to convert narrative passages to dialogue (and vice versa), to write advice to a specific character, to change the point of view of a specific scene, to write a prequel or sequel, and to write diary entries for a specific character before, during, or after the time of the story.

Writing narratives about literature enables students to actively participate in what they are reading. Writing narratives about literature brings students closer to the characters, the plot, and the theme, and serves to involve them in the story. In short, writing narratives about literature is the ideal way to bring about the vital synthesis of language, literature, and composition that is the aim of language arts teaching. See page 144 for a listing of recommended authors and narratives which can be used as foundations or sources for these assignments.

The following prewriting activities are suitable for any of the assignments in writing narratives about literature. These activities are engaging and thought provoking and will produce unique variations on the literature.

Character Comparison

1. As prewriting exercises for all literature, students should use the Character Relationship Graphic Organizer (page 137) and Character Trait Graphic Organizer (page 138) to analyze characters. To relate personally to characters, students should use the Comparison Graphic Organizer (page 136), comparing themselves to one or more characters.
2. Students should fill out a character sketch for one or more characters.

Who, What, Where, When, Why, and How

Answer *who, what, where, when, why,* and *how* for the literature. Summarize the plot. State the theme and give at least three instances from the literature to support the theme.

Conflict Identification

Create a time line of all conflicts from the literature. In chronological order, list conflicts, types of conflict, and how conflicts were resolved.

114 ©2000 Teacher Created Materials, Inc.

Standards and Benchmarks: 1A, 1B, 1C, 1D, 1E, 1G, 1L, 2A, 2B, 2C, 2D, 3A, 3B, 3C, 3D, 3E, 3F, 3G, 3H, 3I, 3J, 3K, 3L

Character Reaction

Description

Write from the point of view of the main character. Write how the main character reacts to the climax of the story.

Prewriting Activities

- Identify the parts of the story: beginning, middle, climax, and end.
- Complete a character sketch of the main character.
- Complete a Comparison Graphic Organizer (page 136) comparing you with the main character.

Writing

Identify the climax from the story or novel. Summarize the climax in a paragraph. Imagine you are the main character and the "climax" occurs. How would you act and/or react?

You may consider Shirley Jackson's "The Lottery," Richard Connell's "The Most Dangerous Game," or any other short story with a potentially life-threatening climax.

Publishing

- Read your rewritten climax to the class.
- Create a diorama of the climax.

Technology Connections

- Word-process the narrative.
- Using a software program, write the climax in the center of the page. Then list and illustrate personal changes to the narrative, based upon what you would do and how you would react.

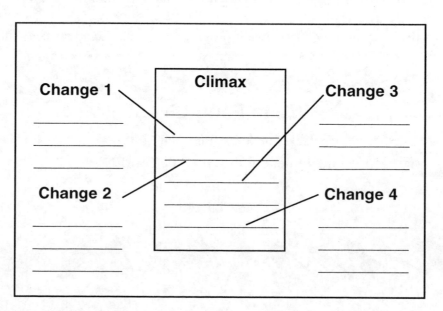

Standards and Benchmarks: 1A, 1B, 1C, 1D, 1E, 1G, 1L, 2A, 2B, 2C, 2D, 3A, 3B, 3C, 3D, 3E, 3F, 3G, 3H, 3I, 3J, 3K, 3L

Right Place, Right Time

Description

Place yourself in the climax of a piece of literature and affect the climax so as to change the story's resolution.

Prewriting Activities

- Identify the parts of the narrative: beginning, middle, climax, and end.
- Free-write on how you could be placed realistically into the story.
- Free-write on what you would do if you were in the same predicament as the main character. Share your responses.
- Cluster the overwhelming feeling you might have if placed in the climax of the narrative.

Writing

Identify the climax from a story or novel. Summarize the climax in a paragraph. Now, imagine that you are in the scene and you must affect the climax in a way that changes the ending. You must describe the circumstances which put you there at the right place and the right time. Describe how your actions, words, or involvement altered the story's resolution. What is your relationship with the main character? Does the main character listen to your suggestions?

Publishing

- Read your narratives to the class.
- Suppose your new narrative has been made into a movie with you as the minor star who has rewritten the narrative to become a blockbuster hit! Create an advertisement for the "movie" version, and be sure to include how your rewrites have made the movie such a smashing success.

Technology Connections

- Word-process the narrative.
- Create a flow chart of the beginning, middle, climax, and end, and include your personal involvement in the narrative.
- Use a graphics program or another software program to create the advertisement.

White Fang Lives!

Jack London's Immortal Story

Rewritten for the GIANT SCREEN

Unites Man and Wolf

As Courage

Triumphs over Death!

Standards and Benchmarks: 1A, 1B, 1C, 1D, 1E, 1G, 1L, 2A, 2B, 2C, 2D, 3A, 3B, 3C, 3D, 3E, 3F, 3G, 3H, 3I, 3J, 3K, 3L

Rewritten Scene

Description
Take one scene from a given piece of literature, place yourself in the scene, and rewrite it.

Prewriting Activities
- Create a time line of scenes from a given piece of literature. (Possible examples might include *The Pearl*, *The Cay*, or "The Necklace.")
- Choose one scene which you find intense and answer *who*, *what*, *where*, *when*, *why* and *how*. Now, you should place yourself in that scene and free-write how you would have acted in the situation. Share personal incidents similar to the scene from literature.
- Identify characters in the scene. Complete the Comparison Graphic Organizer (page 136), comparing yourself and the main character.

Writing
- Assume you have selected John Steinbeck's *The Pearl*. Toward the end of the story, the baby Coyotito is shot and killed. If you were there, how might this tragedy have been avoided?
- What if you had been stranded with Timothy and Phillip from *The Cay*. What would you have done to hasten a rescue?
- In "The Necklace," by Maupassant, what if you were at the party and revealed to Mathilde that the necklace was "paste" (fake). You are now a character in the narrative and will change, or have the ability to change (if you wish), how the narrative unfolds. You may be yourself or another individual, animal, or object.

Publishing
- Write the scene in comic book style. Include illustrations.
- Read the scene to the class.

Technology Connection
- Use a graphics program to create a time line of the new narrative.
- Illustrate the new scene, using a graphics program.

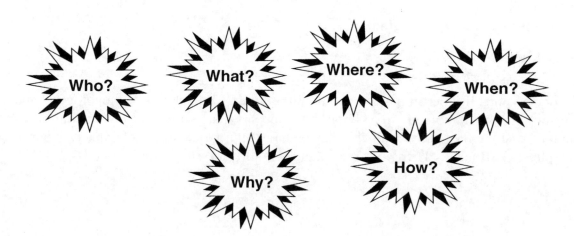

 **Standards and Benchmarks:** 1A, 1B, 1C, 1D, 1E, 1G, 1L, 2A, 2B, 2C, 2D, 3A, 3B, 3C, 3D, 3E, 3F, 3G, 3H, 3I, 3J, 3K, 3L

Interior Monologue

Description

Write an interior monologue from a character's point of view.

Prewriting Activities

- Create a conflict time line for a piece of literature. A conflict time line lists all the conflicts in a particular narrative in chronological order. Not only should the conflicts be listed, but also when and how the conflict was resolved.
- Complete a character sketch for the character presented with conflict.

Discussion

- Discuss interior monologue. Write an interior monologue of a time when you were in the heat of an argument or problem. What were your thoughts?
- Discuss what interior monologues do. Do nonverbal actions and physical actions sometimes give away what we are thinking?
- Discuss how interior monologues benefit narratives.
- Find examples of interior monologues to read and discuss.

Writing

Take an excerpt from literature in which the character is in the middle of conflict. Write an interior monologue putting yourself in the character's mind. Interior monologue is the inner thought of a person, which is revealed only to the character himself or herself. Interior monologue is what we are thinking but do not say orally. Use Edgar Allan Poe's "The Cask of Amontillado." Take the conflict where Fortunato is shackled and walled up in the vaults. Write an interior monologue as he realizes the last brick is in place. Other choices could include Crane's "The Open Boat," Irving's "Rip Van Winkle," or Chopin's "Story of an Hour."

Publishing

Perform interior monologues in costume.

Technology Connections

- Word-process the narratives.
- Videotape yourself, in costume and appropriate setting, reading interior monologue—make cue cards or have the monologue in a "book" so it appears that you are not just reading monologue. You may cast another individual who may be more appropriate as the character—your father, for example, as Fortunato. Then your role changes to director!

Standards and Benchmarks: 1A, 1B, 1C, 1D, 1E, 1G, 1L, 2A, 2B, 2C, 2D, 3A, 3B, 3C, 3D, 3E, 3F, 3G, 3H, 3I, 3J, 3K, 3L

Narration to Dialogue

Description

Rewrite a narrative scene in straight dialogue.

The Cheat Sheet

Shawna yawned and stretched her arms high over her head. Three sharp cracks from Shawna's spine resounded in the silent classroom, and several students giggled. Mr. McGovern's eyes glared around the room; then he placed the test on Gina's desk. Gina breathed, and flipped through the pages, five in all. Mr. McGovern paced the aisles as the class scribbled and erased, the steady click-click of his worn loafers keeping time with the clock. Gina glanced at the clock over the doorway. Thirty minutes left.

She stretched her head from side to side, first with eyes closed, then with eyes open. And that is when she saw it. There, in Shawna's curled left hand was a piece of paper. As Mr. McGovern's clicks approached, Shawna's left-hand stealthily slithered under the desk. Then it returned, and uncoiled the answers.

Gina pulled her chair closer to the desk and the screech sent chills up her, and undoubtedly others' spines. Gina responded to every question—remembering the study sessions with her mother, the after-school help with Mr. McGovern, the reading and rereading of notes, and the memorizing of facts, instead of the trip to the mall, the baseball game, the after-school special. Some of the answers Gina knew, and some she could only try her best to answer.

Shawna finished first, and every class member watched her march to the front and flip the test onto Mr. McGovern's desk. Even Mr. McGovern looked surprised.

As Shawna eased into her seat, she combed her shoulder-length hair with her fingers and drummed her pretty, pink-polished fingertips on the desk.

The bell marking the end of class sounded more like a majorette's whistle signaling the band to begin, and Gina placed her test on the pile in Mr. McGovern's hands. She had finished but had no time to review her answers.

Gina's eyes connected with several of her classmates, a mixture of relief that the test was over and sadness that it was, indeed, over.

Gina didn't know if she could stand seeing Shawna, but she shared lockers with her, and memories, too.

Writing

Rewrite the above narrative using dialogue. Share. Discuss how the narrative changes, and whether the dialogue enhances the narrative.

Technology Connections

- Word-process the dialogues.
- Videotape dialogues with a partner. Create a multi-media presentation integrating dialogue and created characters, or scan images of your characters to use in presentation.

Standards and Benchmarks: 1A, 1B, 1C, 1D, 1E, 1G, 1L, 2A, 2B, 2C, 2D, 3A, 3B, 3C, 3D, 3E, 3F, 3G, 3H, 3I, 3J, 3K, 3L

Dialogue to Narration

Description
Students will rewrite a dialogue scene in straight narration.

Prewriting Activities
From a piece of literature, have students choose one dialogue scene. Students should list what the dialogue reveals about plot, character, setting, and theme.

Study Hall

"I can't believe you." Gina said through clenched teeth. Her brown eyes were dull and fixated on collecting her books needed to complete tonight's homework.

"What's up with that tone, Geenie?" Shawna laughed, her lipstick matching the glow of her cheeks. "Didn't do well on Mr. Mac's test?"

Gina slammed the locker, stuffed her books in her backpack, and paraded down the hall.

"I told you not to waste your time— 'scuse me, *our* time, studying. It was too much material! Half a year crammed into five pages? Get real." Shawna pounced on Gina's heels.

"It's cheating." Gina stopped just outside the school. "It's not fair."

"Mr. McGovern's test wasn't fair. I did nothing wrong. You think I could cram all of his notes and boring lectures and infinity facts onto one measly piece of paper?" Shawna whispered angrily. "Did I ace the test? I have no idea. But at least I have a chance at passing."

"I studied!" Gina cried. "And so did the rest of the class!"

"Waste of time." Shawna laughed wickedly. "Tell me, my friend, how did you do on the test? All that studying worth it?"

Gina didn't answer right away, and Shawna looked pleased. "See? I told you I'd show you how to study. I told you not to waste our time studying. Guess you don't trust me, huh?"

"Trust you? If I had known you were going to show me how to cheat, I . . . well," Gina stopped. "What if you got caught?"

"Never have. Never will." Shawna laughed and strutted down the sidewalk. "Stick with me, Geenie-cakes, and school can be fun!"

Writing
- Discuss whether the friendship will continue or end. Write "Study Hall" only in narration. Share.
- Write a narrative about the next day in Mr. McGovern's class. Be creative. Use the point of view of the teacher, Gina, Shawna, or another classmate. What happens? Share.
- Exchange narratives with a peer group and use the Reader Response Check Sheet (page 126). Revise your narrative, using peer group suggestions and what you feel is necessary. Proofread for accuracy in spelling and punctuation.

Technology Connections
- Word-process the narrations.
- Experiment with font, borders, color, and graphics to create a title page.

Standards and Benchmarks: 1A, 1B, 1C, 1D, 1E, 1G, 1L, 2A, 2B, 2C, 2D
3A, 3B, 3C, 3D, 3E, 3F, 3G, 3H, 3I, 3J, 3K, 3L

Friendly Advice

Description

Advise a character about how to deal with a conflict.

Prewriting Activities

- From a piece of literature, the class should list all conflicts on the chalkboard. Students should copy these in their journals. Next, students should complete a class character sketch.
- Free-write on the topic: If the character were a member of our school, would you be friends with him or her? Why? Share responses.
- Write in your journals about a time you gave someone advice. Describe the circumstance, tell whether your advice was taken and whether your advice assisted or confused the person in his or her dilemma.

Writing

Imagine that you happen across the main character of a story just as a conflict arises:

- What are the circumstances that have placed you in the right place at the right time?
- What will you do or say to the main character to assist him or her in the dilemma he or she faces?
- Does what you do or say affect the plot of the story?

Respond to all the above questions as you give advice to the literature character you have selected as a "good friend." Suggestions of literature to select your character from are Jack London's "To Build a Fire," Scott O'Dell's *Island of the Blue Dolphins*, Wilson Rawls' *Where the Red Fern Grows*, or Esther Forbes' *Johnny Tremain*.

Publishing

Share the narratives with the class.

Technology Connection

Create a Web site of questions based on your characters from literature and the conflicts they face. Provide an e-mail address so advice can be directed directly to these characters! Post on a Web site creatively titled. Share with classes around the country who may have read the same narratives.

(The above suggestion may exceed the technology resources and budget of any given school. If so, try designing the activity on paper without actually creating a "real" Web site.)

 **Standards and Benchmarks:** 1A, 1B, 1C, 1D, 1E, 1G, 1L, 2A, 2B, 2C, 2D, 3A, 3B, 3C, 3D, 3E, 3F, 3G, 3H, 3I, 3J, 3K, 3L

Point of View

Description

Write a narrative scene from the point of view of a minor character.

Prewriting Activities

- List all characters from a piece of literature and identify their roles in the story.
- Identify which character you are most like and give reasons why, including specific examples from the literature.
- Create a character sketch of a minor character. Use what you know about the character to complete the sketch. Create facts if necessary. For example, it sometimes helps to imagine a rich background for your minor character to help flesh out your understanding. The following hints may help you get started.

My minor character has . . .

1. an important brother or sister
2. a mysterious but unrevealed event in his or her past
3. a tragic accident at an earlier age
4. an eccentric father or mother
5. a special ability, skill, or art
6. a history of unusual travel
7. an unusual disability
8. a great sense of courage or honor
9. a great sense of fear of some thing or happening
10. a special culture or language

Writing

Rewrite a narrative scene from the first person point of view of a minor character. How does another character view the situation? Be creative. Take the dog, for instance, in "To Build a Fire" or the Wicked Witch of the West in *The Wizard of Oz*. Tell the story through their eyes.

Publishing

Share the narrative scenes with the class.

Technology Connections

- Word-process the narratives.
- Use clip art, download images, or scan images which represent the characters in the story.

Standards and Benchmarks: 1A, 1B, 1C, 1D, 1E, 1G, 1L, 2A, 2B, 2C, 2D, 3A, 3B, 3C, 3D, 3E, 3F, 3G, 3H, 3I, 3J, 3K, 3L

A Gift

Description

Write a narrative about a valuable object owned by the main character of a piece of literature.

Prewriting Activities

- Complete a character sketch on a main character from a piece of literature.

- List several objects this character might have in his or her possession which have great value—either monetary or sentimental value. Next to each object, state who gave the character the object, why it was given to him or her, and why it is so valuable.

- Write about one object of your own which you find valuable and analyze your own feelings if this object were to be lost.

Writing

The main character has one item he or she values. What is this one item, and why does the main character value it? The object could be a letter, gift, souvenir, book—anything! In your narrative, show how the object comforts or assists the character in overcoming conflict. You may also choose to write from the character's point of view, and write a narrative about the history of your object—how it came into your possession, and what it means to you.

Publishing

Illustrate the valuable object and share narratives.

Technology Connections

- Word-process the narratives.
- Create a thank-you card using a graphics program. Include a thank-you note, written in one strong paragraph.

The History of My . . .

ring?

watch?

bracelet?

small silver box?

pocket knife?

locket?

ornate picture frame?

special book?

napkin ring?

violin?

special pen?

string of beads?

old belt?

small chain?

 **Standards and Benchmarks:** 1A, 1B, 1C, 1D, 1E, 1G, 1L, 2A, 2B, 2C, 2D, 3A, 3B, 3C, 3D, 3E, 3F, 3G, 3H, 3I, 3J, 3K, 3L

Prequel/Sequel

Description

Write a prequel or sequel to a selected piece of literature.

Prewriting Activities

- Define *prequel* and *sequel*. Read an excerpt from a sample short story or narrative.

- As a class, brainstorm ideas for a prequel and sequel. If a short story was used, read the entire piece to see if student predictions were accurate.

- Discuss whether various ideas would or could have made the narrative stronger.

- Choose one piece of literature and identify the parts of the story: beginning, middle, climax, and end.

- Next, write a one-paragraph summary of the beginning and the end.

- Write a plot jot for a prequel and sequel. At least 10 questions should be asked and answered before writing the narrative.

Writing

Write a prequel or sequel to a literature selection. A *prequel* takes place before the story, and a *sequel* is a narrative which takes place after the story. In a prequel, the end must prepare the readers for the actual beginning of the piece of literature. In a sequel, the narrative must begin at the end of the piece of literature. "The Fall of the House of Usher" by Poe would provide a basis for writing a prequel, and Guy de Maupaussant's "The Necklace" may inspire a sequel.

Publishing

- Read the prequel and sequel to the class.

- Create titles for your prequel and sequel.

- Summarize the prequel and sequel and create a book jacket with your summary.

Technology Connections

- Word-process the prequels and sequels.

- Design a cover for the new book using a graphics application. Include a new title, book jacket, general biography of the author, and a summarization of the narrative.

 **Standards and Benchmarks:** 1A, 1B, 1C, 1D, 1E, 1G, 1L, 2A, 2B, 2C, 2D, 3A, 3B, 3C, 3D, 3E, 3F, 3G, 3H, 3I, 3J, 3K, 3L

Dear Diary

Description

Compose diary entries from the main character's point of view.

Prewriting Activities

- From a selected piece of literature, create a time line of scenes from beginning to end.
- Complete a character sketch of the main character.
- Analyze the main character's actions, speech, language, and personality. Find specific examples in the text which reveal these traits.
- Free-write on the topic "What is usually written in a diary?"

Writing

Compose a series of diary entries from the main character's point of view. To brainstorm diary entry topics, pretend you are the main character and are writing in your journal. Cluster, from the main character's point of view, the following words:
- hope
- friend
- vacation
- loneliness

Then, free-write from the main character's point of view responses to the following:

- When I am alone, I like to . . . .
- My favorite relative is . . . .
- The most embarrassing moment I ever had was when . . . .

(Of course, if you think of different words to cluster or free-writing topics, use them!) You do not have to keep your responses related to the plot of the story, but you do need to be consistent with the character.

Publishing

- Handwrite diary entries in the handwriting your character might have.
- Read one diary entry to the class. See if they can guess who you are!

Technology Connections

- Word-process the diary entries. Experiment with appropriate fonts.
- Create a cover for the diary, using creative borders, fonts, clip art, and colors.

Dear Diary,

Standards and Benchmarks: 1A, 1B, 1C, 1D, 1E, 1G, 1L, 2A, 2B, 2C, 2D 3A, 3B, 3C, 3D, 3E, 3F, 3G, 3H, 3I, 3J, 3K, 3L

Reader Response Check Sheet

1. What is the actual narrative about?

   Plot: _____

   Characters: _____

   Conflict (and how conflict was resolved): _____

   Beginning: _____

   Middle: _____

   Climax: _____

   End: _____

2. Does the original narrative show understanding of the actual narrative? What elements of the actual narrative remained the same? _____

   _____

3. How was the actual narrative altered? _____

   _____

4. What was your first impression of the title? How did the title relate to the narrative? _____

   _____

5. Figurative language examples: _____

   _____

6. Sensory imagery examples: _____

   _____

7. Action verbs: _____

   _____

8. Character descriptions: _____

   _____

9. Spelling/Punctuation: _____

10. What would you do to revise the narrative? _____

11. List three strengths of the narrative: _____

   _____

Assessment Rubric

The rubric is weighted at 100%. Ten is the highest single score. Add up numbers to get a total score.

1. All prewriting activities were completed. 10 9 8 7 6 5 4 3 2 1 0	
2. The narrative shows understanding about the actual literature on which the narrative was based. 10 9 8 7 6 5 4 3 2 1 0	
3. The narrative shows evidence of revision and incorporation of reader-response comments. 10 9 8 7 6 5 4 3 2 1 0	
4. The characters are described accurately and are true to the original narrative. 10 9 8 7 6 5 4 3 2 1 0	
5. The parts of the story (beginning, middle, climax, and end) follow sequentially. 10 9 8 7 6 5 4 3 2 1 0	
6. Figurative language, sensory imagery, and strong action verbs contribute to the story. 10 9 8 7 6 5 4 3 2 1 0	
7. Spelling is correct. 10 9 8 7 6 5 4 3 2 1 0	
8. Punctuation is accurate. 10 9 8 7 6 5 4 3 2 1 0	
9. The narrative is creative, unique, interesting, and adds a new dimension to the actual literature. 10 9 8 7 6 5 4 3 2 1 0	
10. The overall presentation meets guidelines. 10 9 8 7 6 5 4 3 2 1 0	
Total Score	

The Short Story

Writing a short story is similar to writing or nonfiction narratives. Realistic characters, descriptive setting, intriguing conflict, stimulating plot, and a theme that readers can identify are still required elements in the short story.

However, the ideas for short stories come from you and your imagination. Short stories are meant to include the reader. The reader knows that the short story is imagined; nevertheless, the events, characters, setting, and conflict are presented so descriptively and so expertly woven as to make the reader think "This could really happen." The short story invites readers to become active participants in the narrative, to empathize with the characters and their problems. Because readers become so involved in the short story, they, too, will hear the underlying message of the narrative—the theme.

Let your short story narratives have your readers struggle to survive and test their own endurance. Let your narratives transport your readers to fantasy worlds. Let your narratives have your readers on the edge of their seats as they attempt to solve the mystery. Let your narratives encourage your readers to experience events they may or may not have experienced.

Writing for Short Story Narratives

The activity pages which follow all contain story outlines that may be used both to analyze the structure of the sample narratives listed with each activity and also as preparation outlines for original short stories to be written by the students.

Publishing and Technology Ideas for Short Story Narratives

1. Word-process short stories.

2. Create a cover for their short story, using a graphics program.

3. Post stories on a personal Web site and invite reader comments.

4. E-mail short stories to family and friends and ask for feedback.

5. Use a video camera and reenact a scene from their short story.

6. Use the Internet to search for magazines, newspapers, etc., that publish student work. Students can e-mail cover letters and short stories and try to get officially published.

7. Download images that represent characters or settings in their narratives.

8. Take photographs of "scenes" from their short stories and create a slide show with captions.

9. Write mystery short stories without revealing the ending, and post them on a Web site. Other students may guess or predict the ending.

10. Create a time line based on their short stories.

Standards and Benchmarks: 1A, 1B, 1C, 1D, 1E, 1G,, 2A, 2B, 2C, 2D, 3A, 3B, 3C, 3D, 3E, 3F, 3G, 3H, 3I, 3J, 3K, 3L

Adventure/Survival

Description

Adventure and survival stories contain physical adventure, with the conflict centering on confrontations with nature, society, and oneself. The setting should be vivid and invigorate the senses so the reader can actually experience the world the characters are facing. First person point of view is the primary choice for adventure/survival narratives. The characters reveal their thought processes and how they solve problems they encounter, which draws the reader into their world. Because the main character is usually alone, he or she undergoes a change, or metamorphosis, by the narrative's conclusion.

Sample Adventure/Survival Narratives

- *Julie of the Wolves* and *My Side of the Mountain* by Jean Craighead George
- *Island of the Blue Dolphins* by Scott O'Dell
- *Hatchet* by Gary Paulsen
- *The Cay* by Theodore Taylor

Writing

- Analyze one or more of the stories above, using the outline which follows.
- Write an original adventure/survival narrative, using the outline below as preparation.

❑ Setting _____

❑ Character(s)

Description at Beginning	Description at Conclusion
1._____	_____
2._____	_____
3._____	_____

How did the main character get into the predicament?_____

Could the predicament have been avoided? How?_____

How does nature play a major role in narrative?_____

❑ Conflict(s) _____

❑ Plot

Beginning: _____

Middle:_____

Climax:_____

End: _____

❑ Theme _____

Publishing and Technology Ideas (See page 128.)

 **Standards and Benchmarks:** 1A, 1B, 1C, 1D, 1E, 1G, 2A, 2B, 2C, 2D
3A, 3B, 3C, 3D, 3E, 3F, 3G, 3H, 3I, 3J, 3K, 3L

Fantasy

Description

Fantasy narratives are escapes into imaginary worlds and give characters extraordinary experiences. Fantasy narratives make one wonder, "Could this really happen?" as settings often begin realistically and characters stumble into another world either similar to or quite different from their own. Fantasy narratives base their success on getting readers to suspend disbelief. Characters, both "real" and imagined, need to be so expertly characterized that both they and the world they inhabit seem as if they could exist. The main characters often travel back to the real world, and the journey into fantasy has almost always taught them something. Therefore, fantasy narratives need a worthwhile theme.

Sample Fantasy Narratives

- *A Wrinkle in Time* by Madeline L'Engle
- *A Wizard of Earthsea* by Ursula LeGuin
- *The Hobbit* by J.R.R. Tolkein

Writing

- Analyze one or more of the stories listed above, using the outline which follows.
- Write an original fantasy narrative, using the outline below as preparation.

❑ Setting _____

❑ Character(s)

Real World	Imaginary World
1._____	_____
2._____	_____
3._____	_____

How does the main character get from the real world to an imaginary world? _____

Why does the character go to an imaginary world? _____

How does the main character return to the real world? _____

What changes does the character go through because of his or her adventure?_____

What does the character do, or how does the character adjust to being back in reality? Will the character ever return to the imaginary world?_____

❑ Language used in the imaginary world _____

❑ Conflict _____

❑ Theme _____

Publishing and Technology Ideas (See page 128.)

Standards and Benchmarks: 1A, 1B, 1C, 1D, 1E, 1G, 2A, 2B, 2C, 2D, 3A, 3B, 3C, 3D, 3E, 3F, 3G, 3H, 3I, 3J, 3K, 3L

Mystery

Description

Unexplainable incidents, mysterious figures, dark and stormy nights all contribute to the success of a good mystery. Suspense—and continued suspense—is necessary in the plot. Clues are presented in the narrative as the character discovers them. Thus, the reader and character are working together to solve the mystery. The character logically assembles the clues and shows how he pieced the clues together to solve the mystery. The setting is vital in a mystery, as is the "crime" or mystery. To entice the reader, the crime is usually presented as early as possible, and the character "stumbles" over this mystery, either becoming a suspect, the next potential victim, or simply entangled in the events. Without figuring out the mystery, the character can't sleep at night.

Sample Mystery Narratives

- *The House of Dies Drear* by Virginia Hamilton
- *Whalesinger* by Welwyn Katz
- Any novel by Christopher Pike, R.L. Stine, or Agatha Christie

Writing

- Analyze one or more of the stories listed above, using the outline which follows.
- Write an original mystery narrative, using the outline below as preparation.

❑ Setting: _____

❑ What is the mystery or crime?_____

❑ Clues: _____

❑ Characters

    1._____   _____

    2._____   _____

    3._____   _____

    How did the main character become involved?_____

    Is the character in any danger? _____

    How will the character find the clues? _____

    How will the character piece together clues to solve the mystery? _____

    What will happen to the perpetrator? _____

    What happens to the character as a result of solving the mystery? _____

❑ Plot

    Beginning: _____

    Middle:_____

    Climax:_____

    End: _____

Publishing and Technology Ideas (See page 128.)

Standards and Benchmarks: 1A, 1B, 1C, 1D, 1E, 1G, 2A, 2B, 2C, 2D, 3A, 3B, 3C, 3D, 3E, 3F, 3G, 3H, 3I, 3J, 3K, 3L

Contemporary Realistic

Description

Contemporary realistic narratives are realistic stories—everything is consistent with contemporary life. The characters, setting, conflicts, and plot could actually happen. Characters in contemporary realistic narratives are presented with real problems: divorce, health issues, race and gender issues, family and school troubles, friendship issues, self-esteem and self-image concerns, to name a few. Realistic short stories are valuable because they allow readers to experience situations in a risk-free environment. They can see what could happen or might happen in certain situations. Contemporary realistic narratives must involve the reader so they can join in the main character's struggle to overcome the conflict and completely empathize with his or her plight.

Sample Contemporary Realistic Narratives

- *Are You There God? It's Me, Margaret* by Judy Blume
- *Dear Mr. Henshaw* by Beverly Cleary
- *After the Rain* by Norma Fox Mazer
- *Scorpions* by Walter Dean Meyers

Writing

Before beginning a contemporary realistic narrative, brainstorm issues that you deal with personally, that have affected your friends, or that concern you. Share your lists with the class. Even the list you and your classmates have brainstormed is probably not exhaustive—any event in real life can be shaped into a story.

Use the following outline as a framework for your own contemporary realistic story.

- ❑ Contemporary topic of narrative: _____
- ❑ Reasons I wish to explore this topic: _____
- ❑ Describe any personal experience with this topic: _____
- ❑ How will you fictionalize this experience? _____
- ❑ Characters: _____
- ❑ Setting: _____
- ❑ Conflict: _____
- ❑ Plot

  Beginning: _____

  Middle: _____

  Climax: _____

  End: _____
- ❑ What feeling do I want my readers to feel at the conclusion of the narrative? Why? _____
- ❑ What do I want my readers to learn from the narrative? _____

Publishing and Technology Ideas (See page 128.)

Standards and Benchmarks: 1A, 1B, 1C, 1D, 1E, 1G, 2A, 2B, 2C, 2D, 3A, 3B, 3C, 3D, 3E, 3F, 3G, 3H, 3I, 3J, 3K, 3L

Reader Response Check Sheet

1. List the elements reflective of the short story type and how they are included in this narrative. (Use the back of this page.)

2. Parts of the story:

   Beginning:_____

   Middle: _____

   Climax: _____

   End: _____

3. Identify:

   Conflict: _____

   How conflict was resolved: _____

4. Identify:

Characters	Believable?	Description
a. _____	_____	_____
b. _____	_____	_____
c. _____	_____	_____
d. _____	_____	_____

5. What is the setting? Could you picture where story took place? Does the setting impact the story? How? _____

6. Figurative language examples:_____

   _____

7. Sensory imagery examples:_____

8. Was the dialogue realistic? True to character description? Essential to the narrative?

   _____

9. Punctuation and spelling: _____

10. Strengths of the story: _____

11. Three suggestions for improvement: _____

    _____

    _____

Assessment Rubric

The rubric is weighted at 100%. Ten is the highest single score. Add up numbers to get a total score.

1. All elements for the particular short story are included in the narrative. 10 9 8 7 6 5 4 3 2 1 0	
2. Characters are realistic and not stereotyped. 10 9 8 7 6 5 4 3 2 1 0	
3. The setting contributes to the story. 10 9 8 7 6 5 4 3 2 1 0	
4. Figurative language and sensory imagery draw reader into the narrative. 10 9 8 7 6 5 4 3 2 1 0	
5. The theme is clear. 10 9 8 7 6 5 4 3 2 1 0	
6. The narrative is original, and the short story is properly sequenced with a beginning, middle, climax, and an end. 10 9 8 7 6 5 4 3 2 1 0	
7. The beginning is intriguing, and the conflict is introduced to draw in the reader. 10 9 8 7 6 5 4 3 2 1 0	
8. The short story shows evidence of revision. 10 9 8 7 6 5 4 3 2 1 0	
9. Spelling and punctuation are correct. 10 9 8 7 6 5 4 3 2 1 0	
10. Final presentation is neat and organized with an appealing title. (Illustrations are optional.) 10 9 8 7 6 5 4 3 2 1 0	
Total Score	

Standards and Benchmarks: 1A

Graphic Organizers

Graphic organizers are useful because they are visual aids that help students plan and organize their thoughts. Graphic organizers help students to "see" their narrative emerge.

❑ **Comparison Graphic Organizer (page 136)**

The Comparison Graphic Organizer allows comparison of similarities and differences between characters, plots, themes, and settings. The similarities are listed where the circles overlap, and the differences are listed where the circles do not.

❑ **Character Relationship Graphic Organizer (page 137)**

The Character Relationship Graphic Organizer helps students to see how characters in their own narratives and literature narratives relate to each other. The names of characters are listed above the line, and their traits are listed below the line in each oval. The arrows pointing away from that character's oval should list an adjective, word, or phrase to show how that character feels about the one in the oval the arrow points to.

❑ **Character Trait Graphic Organizer (page 138)**

The Character Trait Graphic Organizer helps students recognize four traits of one character, and the ovals will contain examples as proof of the particular trait. This graphic organizer may also be used for the theme. Write the theme in the center oval and give four instances from the narrative of how the theme is evidenced.

❑ **Conflict Graphic Organizer (page 139)**

The Conflict Graphic Organizer assists students in determining the central conflict of narratives, shows the effect the conflict has on two characters, tells how the conflict was resolved, and asks for a personal response about the conflict.

❑ **Paragraph Writing Graphic Organizer (page 140)**

The Paragraph Writing Graphic Organizer lets students take one topic and break it down into four separate paragraphs. Students will learn to use this independent clustering technique to recognize how paragraph topics emerge from the main topic.

❑ **Family Tree Graphic Organizer (page 141)**

The Family Tree Graphic Organizer is beneficial when writing narratives about family. Students not only see the shape of their family but also may get useful story ideas from this visual aid.

Comparison Graphic Organizer

(may be used for plots, characters, conflicts, or settings)

Differences

Similarities

Differences

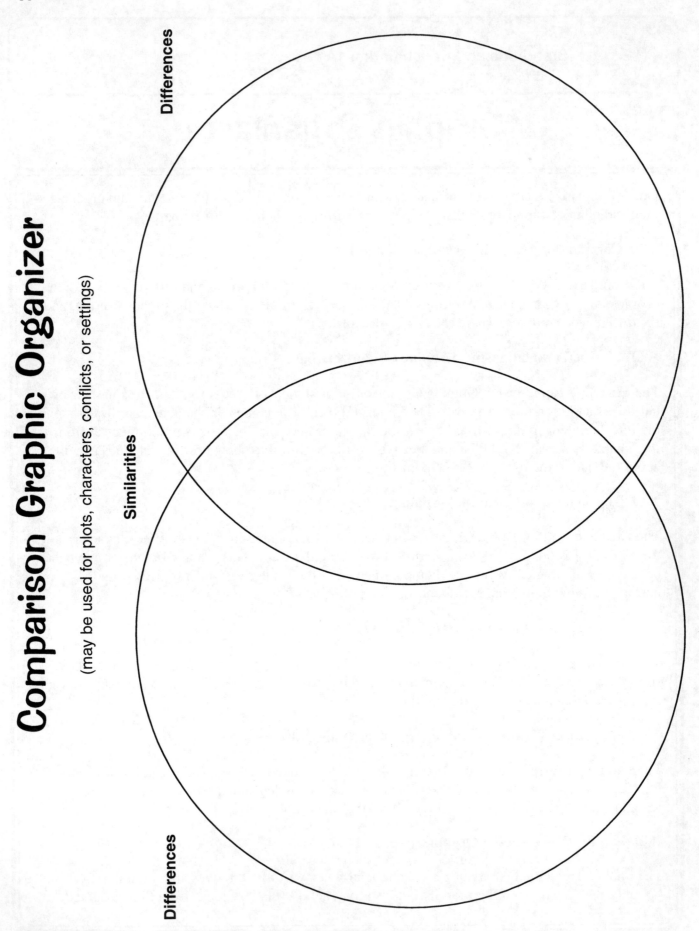

Character Relationship Graphic Organizer

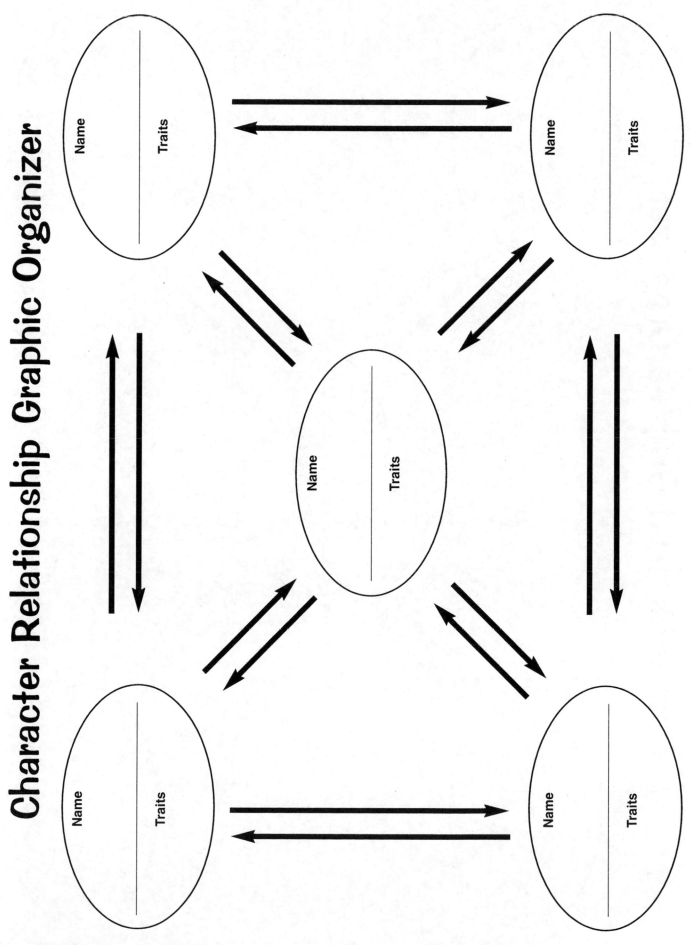

Character Trait Graphic Organizer

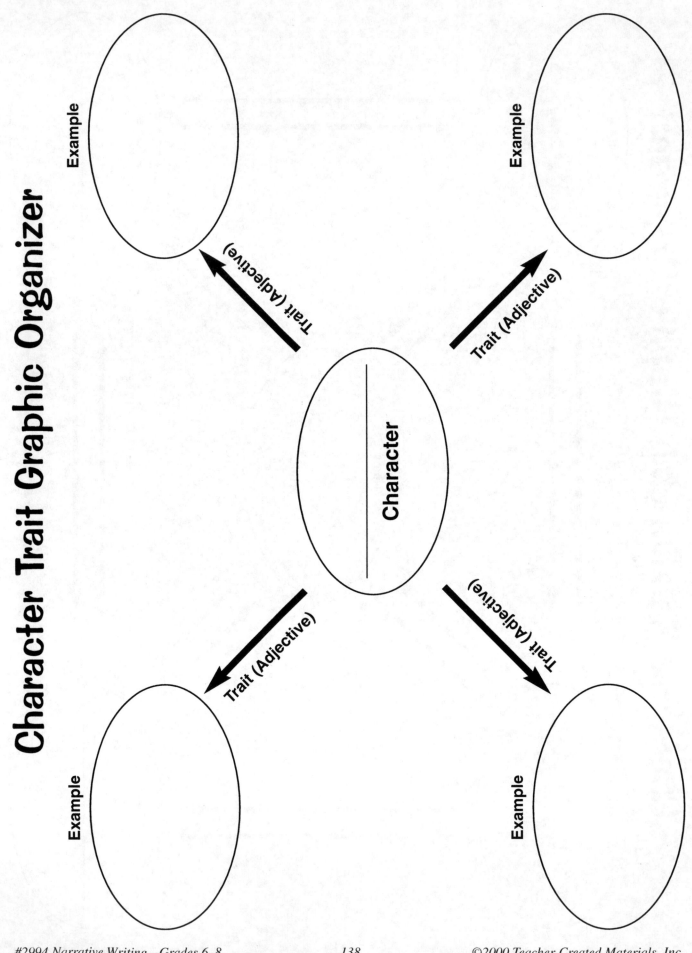

Example

Example

Trait (Adjective)

Trait (Adjective)

Character

Trait (Adjective)

Trait (Adjective)

Example

Example

 ©2000 Teacher Created Materials, Inc.

Conflict Graphic Organizer

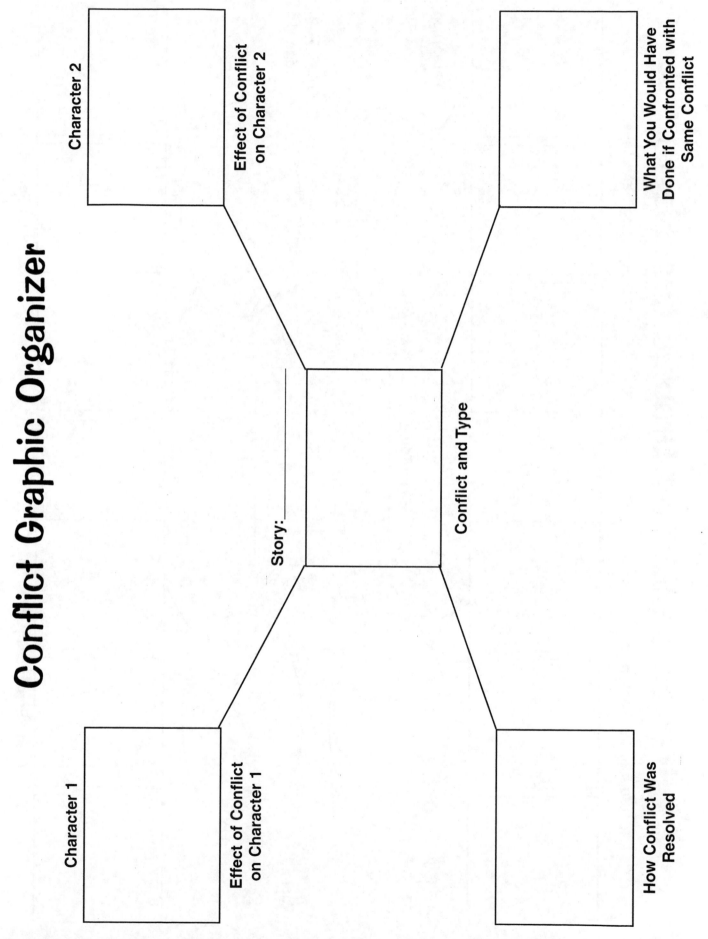

Story: _____

Character 1

Effect of Conflict on Character 1

Character 2

Effect of Conflict on Character 2

Conflict and Type

What You Would Have Done if Confronted with Same Conflict

How Conflict Was Resolved

Paragraph Writing Graphic Organizer

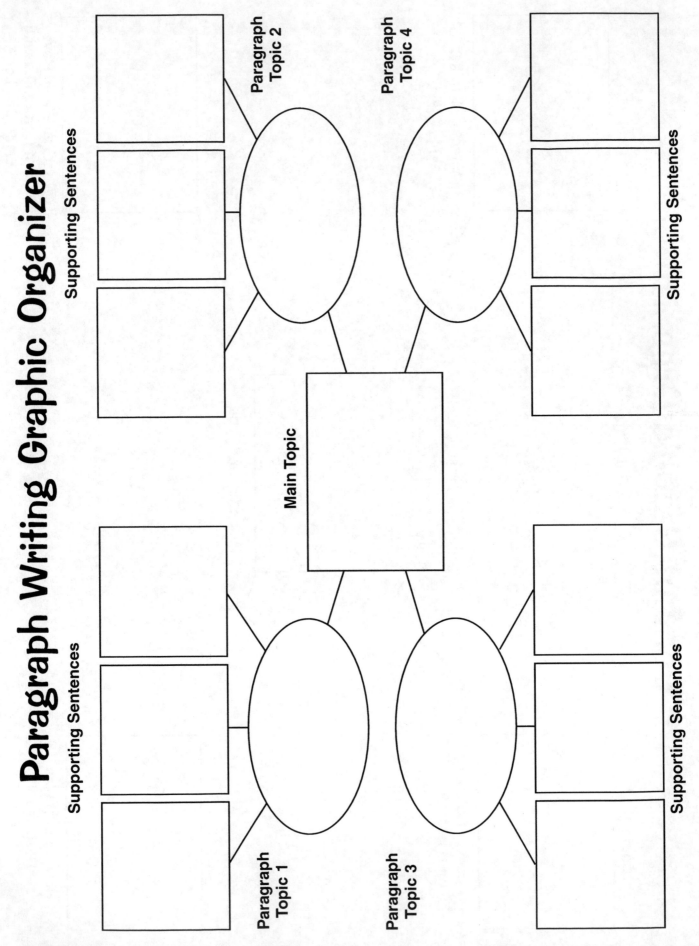

Family Tree Graphic Organizer

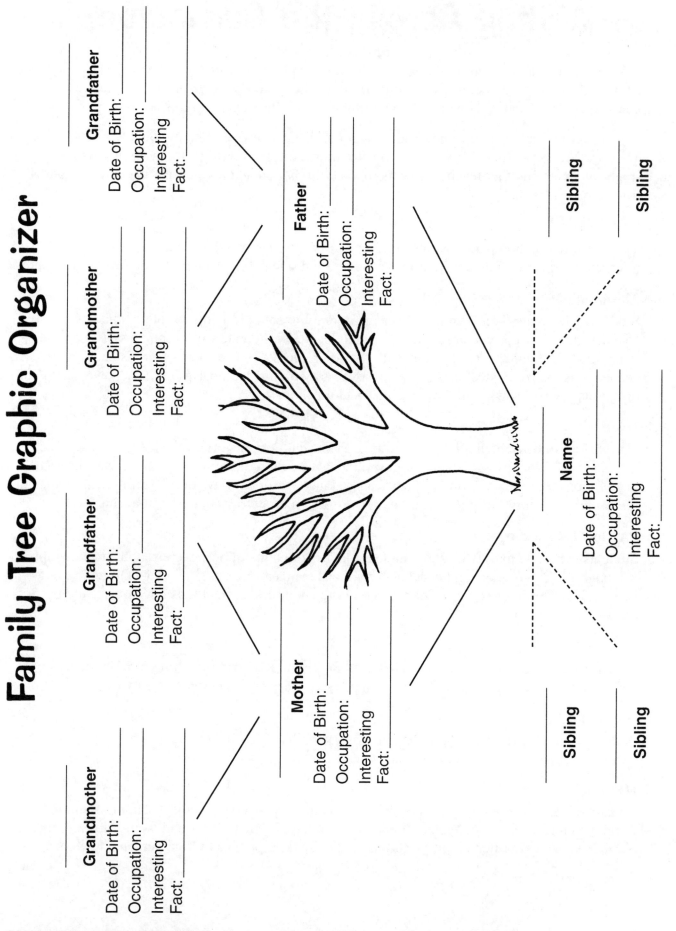

Grandfather

Date of Birth: _____
Occupation: _____
Interesting
Fact: _____

Grandmother

Date of Birth: _____
Occupation: _____
Interesting
Fact: _____

Grandfather

Date of Birth: _____
Occupation: _____
Interesting
Fact: _____

Grandmother

Date of Birth: _____
Occupation: _____
Interesting
Fact: _____

Father

Date of Birth: _____
Occupation: _____
Interesting
Fact: _____

Mother

Date of Birth: _____
Occupation: _____
Interesting
Fact: _____

Name

Date of Birth: _____
Occupation: _____
Interesting
Fact: _____

Sibling

Sibling

Sibling

Sibling

Writing Across the Curriculum

Writing in all subject areas is important because writing is part of our lives. We write to communicate, to share, to inform, to persuade, and to entertain. It is vital to incorporate narrative writing into other disciplines so students realize how effective writing is to get ideas and thoughts across.

The following list of subjects or topic ideas is by no means exhaustive. Share thoughts with colleagues—team up to "share" writing projects to jump-start them. Model the writing process. Encourage students and other teachers to experiment with fiction and nonfiction. Create classrooms that write, and write well.

❏ **Science**

The scientific method parallels the writing process! Research and write narratives, personal or nonfiction, on astronomers, inventors, scientists, and science experiments gone awry—be creative!

❏ **Math**

Students can create their own narratives incorporating math problems for other students to solve. Use the math concept you are focusing on and let students create word problems. (Of course, your students should correctly "solve" the word problem!) Write about business entrepreneurs, accountants, bankers, stockbrokers, analysts, history of "math" (abacus, etc.), why we need math, or the math wizards who think up theories and theorems.

❏ **History**

Narratives can be written about other time periods, cultures, historical events, historical figures, the shaping of countries, changes of government, secession of the South, wars, expansion and exploration, explorers, conquering lands and taking territories, ways of life, prominent women and minorities in history, or writing our "daily" history—narratives about current events.

❏ **Physical Education**

Students can write narratives about athletes, games or competitions, exercise, physical therapists, personal trainers, trainers and coaches for various teams and sports, history of Olympics, how the United States or other countries have fared in the Olympics, current fads in exercise, and benefits of exercise.

❏ **Home Economics**

Students can write narratives about chefs, culinary schools, various cultures, ethnic foods, restaurants, interior designers, fashion designers, or trace fashion trends and styles.

❏ **Industrial Arts**

Students can tell the stories of architects, contractors, and wood workers, or write personal narratives about their own building and constructing.

❏ **Health**

Narratives can be about doctors, nurses, nurse's aides, specialties, medical school, training, latest developments, diseases, cures, or individuals who have battled illness and won or lost the fight. Narratives can be written about nutritionists, dieting, sex, pregnancy, and personal hygiene.

Standards and Benchmarks: 1A, 1B, 1C, 1D, 1E, 1G, 1H, 1I, 2A, 2B, 2C, 2D, 3A, 3B, 3C, 3D, 3E, 3F, 3G, 3H, 3I, 3J, 3K, 3L

Quick Writes

Quick writes are just what their name implies: a short writing assignment enabling students to practice writing under a given time restriction. With quick writes, students will practice gathering information, creating their own prewriting activities on a given topic, organizing thoughts, and presenting these thoughts sequentially. Quick writes give students opportunities to create a narrative, complete with conflict, setting, characters, and theme, in a specific time period. Through practice, students will gain confidence in themselves as writers and in their writing abilities.

Remind students to use the 5Ws +H; the plot jot; or outlines of the beginning, middle, climax, and end as three ways to gather information before beginning. Emphasize the importance of taking a moment to think the story through before beginning. Even if the students do not physically write down any prewriting task, at least they have had a "test-drive."

1. Write a narrative that centers around a door.
2. Write a narrative about a painful memory.
3. Write a narrative about equality.
4. Write a narrative about prejudice.
5. Write about being a child from the point of view of a child.
6. Write a narrative about divorce.
7. Write a narrative about something you had to eat but didn't want to.
8. Write a narrative about a chain-link fence.
9. Write a narrative about the phrase "If at first you don't succeed, try again."
10. Write a narrative about a substitute teacher.
11. Write a dialogue between a clown and a little boy.
12. Write an interior monologue of a person who is told he or she has a terminal illness.
13. Write about a character hiking in the woods. Describe the conflicts this person encounters. You must have a conflict from each type—person vs. person, person vs. machine, person vs. self, person vs. nature, and person vs. society.
14. Write a narrative about an alien who lands in your living room.
15. Write a narrative about writing narratives.
16. Write a narrative about the discovery of a new animal.
17. Write a narrative about the day you were the teacher.
18. Write a dialogue about a conversation you overhead that wasn't meant for you to hear.
19. Write a narrative about a relationship you have with one of your relatives.
20. Write a narrative about the day your home lost electricity.
21. Write a narrative as if you were an "extra" in your favorite television show.
22. Write a narrative about pets.
23. Write a narrative centering around loneliness.
24. Write a narrative about the first day of school.
25. Write a narrative which reflects the phrase "a rolling stone gathers no moss."

Recommended List of Authors and Narratives

- ❏ Baum, L. Frank, *The Wizard of Oz*
- ❏ Bradbury, Ray, *Dandelion Wine*
- ❏ Crane, Stephen, *The Red Badge of Courage*
- ❏ Forbes, Esther, *Johnny Tremain*
- ❏ Frank, Anne, *The Diary of Anne Frank*
- ❏ George, Jean Craighead, *My Side of the Mountain*
- ❏ Hinton, S. E., *The Outsiders*
- ❏ Keller, Helen, *The Story of My Life*
- ❏ Krull, Kathleen, *Lives of the Musicians: Good Times, Bad Times*
- ❏ London, Jack, *White Fang*
- ❏ Morpurgo, Michael, *Joan of Arc*
- ❏ O'Dell, Scott, *The Island of Blue Dolphins*
- ❏ Peck, Robert, *A Day No Pigs Would Die*
- ❏ Rawls, Wilson, *Where the Red Fern Grows*
- ❏ Schaefer, Jack, *Shane*
- ❏ Speare, Elizabeth, *The Witch of Blackbird Pond*
- ❏ Sperry, Armstrong, *Call It Courage*
- ❏ Steinbeck, John, *The Pearl*
- ❏ Taylor, Theodore, *The Cay*

Short Story Authors

- ❏ Richard Connell
- ❏ Stephen Crane
- ❏ Guy de Maupassant
- ❏ Shirley Jackson
- ❏ Edgar Allan Poe